# THE DOG TRAINING HANDBOOK

Sheila Webster Boneham, Ph.D.

*The Dog Training Handbook*
Project Team
Editor: Stephanie Fornino
Copy Editor: Joann Woy
Indexer: Ann Truesdale
Designer: Angela Stanford
Series Designer: Stephanie Krautheim and Mada Design
Series Originator: Dominique De Vito

T.F.H. Publications
President/CEO: Glen S. Axelrod
Executive Vice President: Mark E. Johnson
Publisher: Christopher T. Reggio
Production Manager: Kathy Bontz

T.F.H. Publications, Inc.
One TFH Plaza
Third and Union Avenues
Neptune City, NJ 07753

Printed and bound in China
09 10 11 12 13    3 5 7 9 8 6 4 2

*The Leader In Responsible Animal Care For Over 50 Years!*®
www.tfh.com

# TABLE OF CONTENTS

# 1

# TRAINING BASICS

icture this: You call your dog and he comes running—every single time. He doesn't paw at you and bark when you eat or jump up on everyone who comes near him. He walks calmly and politely on his leash, lies down and stays put when you tell him, and chews only his own chew toys. He's healthy, fit, and happy, a delight to live with, and a credit to his species. Does that sound like your dog or most of the dogs you know? I hope it does! But the sad truth is that far too many dogs are poorly behaved. Why should that be? The long answer is, no doubt, complex and variable, involving biological, psychological, sociological, and other factors. But the short answer is that too few people take the time to train their dogs and to learn how to keep their dogs in optimum health both physically and mentally.

Our popular culture gives us an image of pet dogs as hilariously naughty, and at the same time, miraculously self-trained. Dogs run amok in the movies, knocking over Christmas trees, shredding furniture, and otherwise wreaking havoc, and people react by doing nearly everything imaginable—except training the dogs! On the other hand, stray dogs show up on doorsteps knowing how to do everything but bake a cake. And the two images work together to imply that some dogs are just good and some not so good—a suggestion that all too many dog owners seem to have taken to heart. I'm sorry to burst the Benji bubble, but that's not the way it works outside the movies.

Dogs come to us with many virtues and natural talents. Ten thousand years of mutual evolution and interdependence have enabled our two species to live together with varying degrees of understanding, harmony, and love. But that doesn't mean that dogs instinctively know how to behave the way we want them to. Let's face it, the young of our own species have to be taught to behave themselves. If children aren't self-training, why do so many people seem to think dogs should be? So despite what Hollywood may suggest, your dog wasn't born knowing what you want him to do, and you weren't born knowing how to train your dog.

*Training will help a good dog become a great dog, regardless of size. Small dogs, like this Papillon, are every bit as capable of learning as are their larger cousins.*

Many factors influence how well your dog learns. The methods and tools you use for training affect your dog's ability to absorb the lessons, as does your attitude. Nutrition, health, grooming, and exercise also affect your dog's behavior and his ability to learn. That's why I take a "whole life" approach to teaching you to train your dog. We'll explore these and other influences throughout this book. But first, let's define training, reveal some truths about which dogs can be taught, and see how your dog—and you—can benefit from training.

## WHAT IS TRAINING, ANYWAY?

No matter his age, your dog is always learning, and anything he does more than two or three times will become a habit, whether you like it or not. Training is essentially the process of encouraging

### Your Dog's Right to Be Trained

Lack of basic training can be a death sentence. It's the number-one reason why people get rid of their dogs, and more dogs are turned over to shelters and euthanized for poor behavior than for any other reason. Poor behavior is nearly always caused by lack of training and socialization. People are to blame, but dogs pay the price. Your dog wasn't born knowing what you want, but he was born with the ability to learn. Training is love. It can save your dog's life.

your puppy or dog to form habits you want him to have. It's easier and faster to prevent bad habits and encourage good ones than to try to eliminate bad ones once they're established.

Some habits govern your dog's behavior whether you are present or not. For example, once he's trained and mature enough to control his basic impulses, your dog won't potty in the house or chew on the carpet, regardless of whether you're watching him. Training also develops your dog's habit of following directions. You teach him what a command means, and then when you say it, he does it. I will show you how to motivate your dog to learn and do what you tell him through positive methods of reinforcement.

I will also encourage you to learn as much as possible about dogs in general, your dog's breed or breeds, and your individual dog. If you want your dog to learn what you want from him, you must communicate what you want so that it makes sense to him. Understanding is, after all, a two-way street.

Obedience training is the foundation on which all other training and learning rest. Whether you plan to compete for multiple titles to demonstrate your dog's versatility or you just want a well-mannered companion, training gives you the means to tell your four-legged friend what you want.

## CAN ALL DOGS BE TRAINED?

Most healthy dogs can be trained, although not all of them will excel at learning. Many factors affect your dog's ability to learn and retain information. In Chapter 3, I talk about how exercise, safety, nutrition, health care, and grooming influence training and what you can do to enhance the positive effects and minimize the negative. There are rare dogs for whom learning is especially difficult due to physical, mental, or emotional factors, but most dogs are avid learners if you communicate clearly and provide motivation.

And don't worry—you can indeed teach an older dog new tricks. Many an adult dog turned over to a shelter or rescue program because of problem behaviors has learned to behave just fine in his new home. So if your dog's education has been neglected in the past, don't despair! Although sooner is better, older dogs are often eager learners.

**Training and Teaching**

Although technically "training" and "teaching" are a bit different, I use the terms interchangeably in this book. I want my dogs to think as well as obey, and I want them to understand what I mean when I tell them to do things. I want my dogs to respond quickly to commands but not as unhappy automatons. I want you to have a dog who responds to you with bright eyes and a wagging tail that say "Yes, yes, I got that. Now what?"

*Training helps to build the confidence a dog needs to be a self-assured, mannerly companion and community member.*

## Your Dog Is Always Learning

Training doesn't occur in a vacuum, and your dog doesn't learn just during his once-a-week obedience class or the half hour you set aside each evening for training. The fact is, your dog is learning all the time, at least when he's awake. Your dog is learning when you feed him, walk him, introduce him to your neighbor, when you get busy and ignore him, when you pet him, and when you don't. He's even learning when you aren't there! So be careful to help him learn the things that will enhance his life and enable him to live successfully with you.

## WHAT'S IN IT FOR YOUR DOG?

A dog who has been trained with love, kindness, and clarity is secure and happy. A lot of "nervous" dogs are nervous because they just never know what's expected of them. Let's face it—we humans have enough trouble understanding one another. How can our dogs understand what we want if we don't teach them?

Here's something to consider as well: If you were suddenly unavailable to care for your dog and he needed a new home, is he well enough behaved to be welcomed into a new home? Or is he a little brat with poor social skills? If nothing else motivates you to train your dog, keep in mind that bad behavior is the number-one reason that dogs lose their homes and end up in shelters, where many of them die. Even if you are willing to live with a bratty dog, your dog deserves to learn the basic manners that may someday save his life.

Training gives your dog the essential information he needs to do what you want and avoid doing what you don't want. Training also establishes you as a leader deserving of respect because you provide guidance, protection, and all the good things in life. Knowing that he can rely on you will make your dog more confident in you and in himself. It will also, of course, make him a better-behaved pet and a better member of his community.

## WHAT'S IN IT FOR YOU?

Dog training is good for dog owners as well as for dogs. The most obvious benefit is a better-behaved dog, and that's probably what you're after as you begin or continue your training journey. Training also gets you up and moving—but there's more.

For one thing, there is love. And those of us who love dogs often love them passionately, as full-fledged family members and best friends. As a result, it's tempting to think of them as "fur people" who just happen to have more hair and more legs than we have. Our entertainment media support this view, showing us self-made supercanines who train themselves and express human thoughts and motives through the miracle of special effects. Movie dogs are cute, but thinking of dogs as furry four-footed little people does an enormous disservice to dogs themselves and to our ability to understand and interact with them effectively. One of the benefits of training, then, is the knowledge you will gain about dogs in general and your dog in particular. You will have many opportunities to laugh at your dog and—most likely—at yourself. As your dog learns and becomes more reliable, you will experience the satisfaction and pride that come with accomplishment.

*Most dogs are eager to learn. It's our job to help them learn the right things and make our meaning clear.*

A popular adage among dog lovers asks "Let me be the sort of person my dog thinks I am." Training your dog is a big step on the path to that worthwhile goal. So let's begin!

# Chapter 2

## NATURE

### Dogs Will Be Dogs

Dogs will be dogs—thank goodness! I've heard people say that their dogs are "almost human," and of course they mean it as a compliment. However, dogs by definition possess generous doses of many noble attributes that most humans can only aspire to. Your dog will stand by you when the going gets tough, and he will love you freely, without calculating your net wealth or social standing. This doesn't mean that dogs are perfect—one of the biggest mistakes that pet owners make is to discount the nature of the dog as an intelligent being who, like all humans, is concerned about his own well-being.

Knowing a bit about your dog's perception of the world and his place in it will help you understand and direct his behavior better.

## THE SOCIAL CANINE

Dogs are social animals. They need companionship to lead emotionally and mentally healthy lives. They certainly need shelter, food, health care, and exercise, but most importantly, they need to love and be loved. Dogs are not meant to live solitary lives.

Most dogs enjoy the company of other dogs. They form friendships. They play together. Some dogs sleep cuddled up together or side by side. They touch one another in various ways that show dominance, submission, concern, affection, and love. Anyone who doesn't think that dogs live a rich emotional life hasn't carefully watched the interaction among dogs or between dogs and other animals.

Your dog relies on you not just for his basic needs but also for some, if not all, of his emotional needs. And if you have other pets, they help to satisfy your dog's need for social interaction. If your dog is the only nonhuman member of your household, then you are his pack—his family. Isolating him in a kennel or on a chain, or ignoring him, is cruel—it's the canine equivalent of solitary confinement. What's the point of having a dog if he isn't part of your life?

On the other hand, your dog is not a little person in a furry coat. No question, he was born with a genetic heritage forged over thousands of years to make us

*Dogs are highly social animals who live a rich emotional life when socialized with people and other animals.*

want to love him and live with him. His looks, his abilities, and the friendship he willingly gives us help him connect with us. But your dog's heritage also includes physical and mental traits that make him supremely canine. If we pretend that he's human, we not only demean what it is to be a dog, but we miss out on the rewards of seeing a member of another species for what he really is. It's unfair to your dog and to you, and it limits communication and understanding between the two of you.

## Learning to Play Well With Others

Like all social animals, dogs must learn how to behave around others of their own kind, and in modern society, other kinds as well. Puppies are born with the ability to learn to communicate with and understand others and to exhibit good manners, but they do have to learn these skills. In a normal situation, a pup learns from his dam (mother) and siblings during his first few weeks. But that's just the beginning.

The process of learning to get along socially with others is called

*socialization*, a critical part of your dog's development. We'll discuss how you can help your puppy or dog become fully social later in this book. For now, be aware that nature provided your dog with the inclination to play well with others. It's up to you to give nature a hand.

## The Social Hierarchy

When multiple dogs live together, they normally organize themselves into a *dominance hierarchy* in which each individual ranks higher or lower in relation to each other animal. The socially dominant "top dog" in the hierarchy is the *alpha*; in mixed-sex packs there is usually an alpha dog (male) and an alpha bitch (female). Social status is acquired primarily by force of personality, not gender, age (among adults), or even size and strength. I grew up with a "pack" that included a male Irish Wolfhound, female Scottish Deerhound, female mixed breed, and two Chihuahuas, one of each sex. It was quite a sight when the big guys kowtowed to the Chihuahua bitch, who was the undisputed alpha animal.

*Puppies learn a lot about how to play well with others from their siblings.*

### *The Alpha's Role*

In theory, the alpha controls the resources. In the wild, the alpha (or alpha pair) eats first and takes the best parts of a kill. He sleeps in the best spot. He may play with the other pack members, but there is a line of respect that his subordinates cross at their own peril.

The domesticated alpha has similar rights, although he should defer to human authority. He "owns" the toys, although he may let the other dog play with them. He sleeps on the "best" dog bed or the couch (if you allow him to), while the others sleep in less desirable spots. He has the right to lead the way through doors and gates and to be in front on walks. Again, though, all this is theoretical, and if status is well defined, the alpha may be pretty relaxed about these "rules." Status is often fluid as well, with one dog more dominant in the house and another more dominant outdoors. Individual rankings can also change over time as dogs

## Safety for Kids and Dogs

Kids and dogs—what a wonderful combination. Usually. But harmony between the two doesn't come automatically, and a tragic number of children are bitten every year, most commonly by their own family dogs. Fortunately, almost all bites can be prevented.

Young puppies play roughly and have sharp teeth and claws. Their instincts and their early learning have taught them to use their little needle teeth and toenails in play, so they have to learn to keep their teeth and paws off people, especially children. Kids also have to treat dogs with kindness and respect. They have to be taught not to pull soft doggy ears or fur or poke bright doggy eyes. Although some dogs will put up with an amazing amount of abuse from a child, it's not fair or realistic to expect your pooch to take whatever a child dishes out. Here are a few simple steps you can take to keep your child from being bitten:

- Teach your dog and your child to interact respectfully with the other.
- Train and socialize your dog thoroughly.
- Alter (spay or castrate) your dog—the reduction in sex hormones reduces aggression and lowers the risk of biting in both male and female dogs.
- Supervise all interaction between your young dog and young children, and be ready to intervene immediately. With older children and dogs, use good judgment based on individuals, not their ages.
- Learn to read your dog. Dogs almost never bite without warning, but people often fail to get the message.
- Discourage rough play. It almost always results in someone getting hurt or frightened or both.
- Teach your child never to tease a dog, pretend to bark or growl at one, try to take things away from a dog, or disturb a dog who is sleeping, eating, or caring for puppies.
- Teach your child not to approach strange dogs without permission from the owner. If given permission, teach her to approach the dog slowly and quietly and let the dog sniff her hand before petting.

age or their health changes, and when a new dog arrives or a dog leaves, there will nearly always be some reorganization.

## Characteristics of the Alpha

A true alpha is a benevolent overseer, confident, with no need to throw his weight around. Alpha wannabes, on the other hand, are often insecure about their status and prone to bullying and quarreling. (In that respect, dogs are not unlike people!) Although the possibility of a fight always exists when two living creatures are together, dominance among dogs is usually established through ritualized behaviors, not combat. Staring is dominant, averting the eyes is submissive. Mounting outside of mating is dominant, being mounted is submissive. Placing one or both front paws on another dog's neck or shoulder is dominant, allowing one's neck or shoulder to be pawed is submissive. Submission is also signaled by lying down, rolling belly up, urinating, and looking away from a stare.

Left to their own devices, dogs of equal dominance may fight for a higher position in the pack, but ultimately one of them must either give in (at least for a while) or leave. In a human-controlled environment, however, voluntary departure isn't usually an option, and if two equally matched and ambitious canines are forced to live together, they may fight.

*Your job as pack leader is to reinforce pack harmony.*

Pack status in relation to humans sometimes becomes a problem when a puppy or dog lives with children. The adolescent canine, like a human teenager, has to figure out where he fits into his social group, and some older dogs aspire to higher status within the group. Such dogs may challenge a child's position in the pack. The three most important things you can do to keep such challenges from escalating are to have your dog altered (to reduce hormone levels and remove the urge to procreate), teach your dog and your child to respect one another, and supervise all interaction between your dog and your child, especially while either one of them is young.

### Can Alphas Be "Appointed"?

You can't "appoint" an alpha for your pack. Even if you think that Bertha the Big Dog should be alpha and Bingo the Little Dog should be subordinate to her, Bertha and Bingo may have different ideas. Dogs aren't democratic, and they don't vote for alpha. They establish their relative ranking through ongoing interaction. Each dog's breed traits and individual personality will play a part. In some breeds, most dogs get along well with other dogs, and establishing pack order is a relatively uneventful process. In other breeds, members of the same sex may not do well together, and establishing and maintaining the pack order may be more difficult. A few breeds are generally antisocial with other dogs of either sex.

Unfortunately, people often create or increase tension among their dogs by expecting them to live by human ideals of equality and "fairness" or by imposing human ideas about which one should be top dog. Your human children may insist on having equal shares of all the goodies, but dogs live by a hierarchical system in which the higher-ranking member of the pack gets the best and the biggest, and the lower-ranking members accept whatever is left. The dogs themselves will determine their relative ranks, no matter what you think.

### Your Role in the Hierarchy: Reinforce Pack Harmony

You can reinforce harmony among multiple dogs by paying attention to their interaction and accepting their hierarchy. Observe your dogs together. Does one dog seem to have the right-of-way when others are in his way? Does one take bones and toys away from the other but not vice versa? The clues can be quite subtle when dogs get along well, but if you are observant, you should have an idea of which dog goes first, controls resources, and in general seems to dominate in dog-to-dog interactions. That is your alpha. If you have more than two dogs, each will occupy a specific position relative to each other dog, and no two dogs will hold precisely equal status. The distinctions can be very subtle, though, especially if the individuals have no "political" aspirations and prefer to simply live and let live.

Once you figure out who outranks whom, you can reinforce pack harmony through little everyday actions. Feed the alpha first, then the other(s). (I don't mean let the alpha finish before feeding the others, just feed in that order.) If you're handing out treats,

give the alpha his first. If there's only enough for one, give it to the alpha. If you buy a new toy, give it to the alpha. If the alpha wants to be petted, he gets priority. Does that mean that only your dominant dog should get cookies and toys? Of course not. You are the ultimate alpha (more about that in a moment), so you make the final decision. Just remember that insisting that your dogs take turns being first, or share and share alike, can demean the alpha animal in the eyes of the other pack members and encourage wannabes to challenge him. The resulting tension will make it more difficult for your dogs to focus on what you want them to do and may escalate enough to result in fighting among them.

*Dogs usually get along better if we don't try to impose human notions of fairness and equality on them.*

That said, here's the most important point to remember: To live happily, whether with one dog or five, people need to hold higher status in the pack than all the dogs *from the canine perspective.* You know, of course, that you outrank your dog (at least I hope you do). But your dog may not be so sure. For instance, what do you do if your dog stares at you, barks, and points his moist little nose at the biscuit box? Do you hop up and get him a goody? What if he's blocking your path? Do you go around him? What if he's snuggled up in your favorite chair? Do you let him stay there while you sit on the floor? If you answered yes one or more times, your pooch

*Dogs have an instinct to forge social bonds with other creatures.*

may think he's the household alpha or at least has a chance to move up the ladder.

It's relatively easy to reassert your status in most cases, and you can and should do so without getting excited or "tough." Remember—the alpha is a benevolent dictator. Dog wants a biscuit? Have him do something you want him to do—lie down, roll over, sit, whatever. Then, if you want to give him a biscuit, make it your idea and treat it as a reward. If your dog has already filled his calorie quota for the day, reward him for obedience with a belly rub or a quick game of fetch the toy instead. If he's in your path, tell him to move and keep walking the way you want to go. He needs to move for you. Same deal with your chair—the alpha gets the prime real estate, so he needs to move for you, not the other way around. (Of course if he's old, sick, or just not a challenging type, you can choose to allow him to stay put—as long as it's your choice and not his.)

## YOUR DOG'S INSTINCTS

Your dog's behavior is based almost entirely on either learning or instinct. (Abnormal behaviors can be caused by illnesses, chemicals, head injuries, or other outside influences.) What your dog learns after you bring him home is, of course, up to you. And don't forget that, regardless of his age, he has already learned a few things before he joined your family.

## Understanding Canine Instincts

*Instincts* can be thought of as preprogrammed behaviors or drives that are the result of many generations during which certain behaviors have supported survival of the individual and the species. Understanding these drives will help you train your dog to do what you want and help you anticipate, prevent, and manage problem behaviors. Believe me, your dog studies you with intense interest and understands a lot about your behavior. He also uses his knowledge to his advantage, and there's no reason you can't return the favor. Besides, dogs are much more interesting if we see them not as furry reflections of ourselves but as intelligent, highly motivated creatures with their own needs, interests, and emotions.

*The instinct to hunt for food is highly developed in all canines, wild and domestic. This Beagle is hunting for the lunchmeat.*

*Dogs have the urge to keep their sleeping and eating quarters clean.*

## Instincts Shared by Most Dogs

Some instincts are common to all healthy dogs, regardless of breed. The development of separate breeds of dogs resulted not only in the different physical appearances of modern canines but also the enhancement or suppression of various instincts in different breeds. That's why some breeds or mixes of those breeds are more or less likely to chase and kill other animals, carry things in their mouths, guard home and hearth, be wary of strangers, or welcome one and all.

Whether your dog is a tiny lapdog or a huge guard dog, he has inherited genes that provide him with certain instincts in smaller or larger helpings.

### Social Instinct

The instinct for which we can be most thankful is the instinct to forge social bonds with other creatures. Dogs thrive in the company of others, and by nature, they live in a pack, traits that no doubt helped them establish a bond with humans some 10,000 years ago.

## Hunting and Chasing Instincts

Most dogs have, in varying degrees, the instinct to hunt and kill. For a modern pet, this may be expressed by beating up squeaky toys and stuffed teddy bears or by killing chipmunks and other critters in the yard. The urge to chase moving things is also closely linked to hunting, and in some types of dogs—particularly sight hounds, terriers, and many herding dogs—it's practically irresistible.

Hunting and chasing instincts can be channeled into safe and useful directions through training and management, although controlling these drives can certainly be a challenge in some cases.

## Cleanliness Instinct

Closely tied to the hunting instinct is the urge to roll in ghastly stinky things—not what most of us want in (or on!) a couch companion but clearly a sensuous delight for our dogs. However, dogs do have the urge to keep their sleeping and eating quarters clean. Granted, "clean" is a relative term. Your dog isn't likely to be bothered by a little dust and dog hair, and he probably has a more generous appreciation for ripe smells than you do. However, healthy dogs raised in clean environments and trained with patience and care are more amenable to housetraining because of their instinct not to potty where they live.

*The bond between people and dogs is strengthened by mutual respect and understanding, regardless of breed or mix.*

**Selective Breeding**

Selective breeding is the practice of choosing to mate a male and female with as many desirable characteristics and as few undesirable characteristics as possible in hopes of improving the overall quality of the next generation.

### Reproduction Instinct

The instinct to reproduce is very strong in unaltered (unspayed and uncastrated) dogs, but you are in control of that one. Indeed, some of the canine behaviors that people find most obnoxious are easily eliminated or controlled by altering, especially when the surgery is done before the dog reaches sexual maturity. Altered dogs of both sexes are much less likely to bite, fight, mount, hump, or mark with urine.

## WHAT WAS YOUR DOG BRED TO DO?

Have you ever wondered why the domestic dog comes in so many breeds with so many sizes, colors, forms, attitudes, and special skills? It's a question every current or future dog owner should consider, because this marvelous variety is entirely the result of human intervention in canine breeding. From the diminutive Chihuahua to the massive Mastiff, they are all members of the same species: *Canis familiaris*. Left to select their own mates, dogs would pay no attention to breeds, and after a number of generations of random breeding, their descendants would lose the very specific traits that characterize individual breeds. In fact, around the world, dogs who regularly breed without human intervention all resemble one another, typically weighing in at about 30 to 40 pounds (13.6 to 18.1 kg) and sporting a moderately short coat, upright ears, and loosely curved tail.

### Selective Breeding

*Canis familiaris* forged a bond with our own species thousands of years ago, and we in turn realized that these four-legged animals who wandered into the light of our fires could help us in many ways and also be our friends. Human beings also learned early on that specific traits could be intensified in successive generations by controlling which animals mated with one another. This process of *selective breeding* resulted eventually in breeds of dogs suited to people's many purposes—hunting, guarding, controlling livestock, entertaining and pulling and carrying loads. In the modern world, dogs continue to fill these and other functions, although the job of being a companion is undoubtedly the dog's chief job today, at least in Western societies.

### *How Selective Breeding Affects Your Dog*

So what does selective breeding have to do with training and living with *your* pet dog? Why should you care that his ancestors pulled badgers from burrows or retrieved large dead birds all day in a cold drizzle or pulled sleds across vast plains of snow? You just want a reasonably well-behaved pet to pal around with when you get home from work, a reliable companion for your kids—a loyal and loving playmate, right?

Temperament

Temperament refers to a dog's fundamental tendency to display friendliness, reserve, aggression, stability, and other traits.

Here's the cold, uncomfortable truth: The majority of dogs who lose their homes do so because of normal and predictable behaviors that their owners fail to understand and channel through training, exercise, and appropriate activities. People too often focus on appearances, but it's the inner dog with whom we live. Whether your canine is purebred or a mixed breed, your life with him will make more sense if you understand the behavioral traits of his ancestors (or suspected ancestors).

## Dog Breed Groupings

The more you know about your dog's breed or breeds, the better for you and your dog. Your understanding will pay big dividends in training and in everyday life. Your terrier's inclination to tunnel through your tulips and your working dog's desire to keep strangers out of your home and yard will suddenly make sense. On the other hand, I've seen retrievers who don't like to get their paws wet and toy dogs who would no sooner settle onto someone's lap than play the fiddle. Your dog is an individual, so learn about his relatives, but observe and respect his own strengths and quirks.

Dog breeds can be grouped together using various criteria. I am using the groups system currently recognized by the American Kennel Club (AKC). The AKC categorizes dog breeds into seven groups based more or less on function, although there are some problems with this system. Some placements don't make much sense—the Standard Poodle, for instance, is classed as a Non-Sporting breed, although Poodles were developed and still function as retrievers for hunters of game birds. In addition, many breeds have characteristics that could place them in more than one group—the Dachshund is classified as a hound, for example, but has many traits in common with terriers. The AKC does not recognize all the established breeds, so you may have to look to a different registry to see how your dog's breed is classified. In addition, some groupings put together breeds with very little in common. Still, the AKC groups are a reasonable place to begin.

Now, let's take a look at some of the very general traits that typify canines of different kinds and see what those traits might mean as far as training your dog is concerned.

### The Herding Group

- **Original Purpose:** Gathering livestock together and moving them from place to place.
- **Size:** Herding breeds range in size from the dainty Shetland Sheepdog and the short-of-stature Corgis to the imposing Bouvier des Flandres.
- **Personality and Temperament:** Herding dogs tend to be very intelligent, quick, agile, high-energy dogs who can think on their feet. Some herding dogs are workaholics who live to work, while others are more easygoing and prefer their sheep with mint sauce. Personalities also range from very soft and sensitive to fairly tough, so if your dog is a member of the Herding Group (or has a herding breed in his mix), research the particular breed for better insights.

*The Shetland Sheepdog belongs to the Herding Group.*

*Knowing what his ancestors were designed to do will give you a better understanding of your dog's personality and behavior. As a hunting breed, this Weimaraner will need lots of exercise every day to use up his abundant energy.*

- **Trainability:** Some herding breeds, like the Australian Shepherd and Border Collie, are known for their trainability (as well as their high energy and need to work), while others are a bit more independent.
- **Breed Examples:** The Herding Group includes most of the breeds developed to work with livestock, although a few breeds that traditionally have worked with stock are classed in other groups (the Rottweiler in the Working Group, for example, or the Norwegian Elkhound in Hounds). Specific breeds include the Australian Shepherd, Australian Cattle Dog, Bearded Collie, Border Collie, Bouvier des Flandres, Cardigan Welsh Corgi, German Shepherd Dog, Old English Sheepdog, Pembroke Welsh Corgi, and Shetland Sheepdog.

### The Hound Group

The Hound Group could arguably be split into two groups: sight hounds and scent hounds.

### Sight Hounds

- **Original Purpose:** Sight hound breeds have been used for thousands of years to run down game that they find by sight.
- **Size:** The sight hounds range in size from the compact Whippet to the majestic Irish Wolfhound, the tallest of dogs.

*The Beagle is a member of the Hound Group.*

- **Personality and Temperament:** Most sight hounds are quiet household companions who love their creature comforts, but outdoors they are prone to sudden bursts of incredible speed, and they can cover vast distances in no time flat. In fact, sight hounds are the fastest dogs in the world.

  These dogs spot their prey visually, and once they do so, their high prey drive makes the urge to chase irresistible. This means that a sight hound must be leashed at all times when not securely confined by walls or a fence. When hunting, the long-legged, lean sight hounds hunt alone, in pairs, or in packs and must think for themselves once loosed on their prey.

- **Trainability:** The traditional work of sight hounds required them to hunt down their prey alone or in pairs or small packs, making their own decisions without human direction. They retain the desire to work independently, so to train them you have to provide motivation.

- **Breed Examples:** Sight hounds include the Afghan Hound, Borzoi, Greyhound, Saluki, and Whippet.

### Scent Hounds

- **Purpose:** Scent hounds are designed to locate and track their quarry by scent.
- **Size:** Scent hounds range in size from the diminutive Miniature Dachshund to the sofa-sized Bloodhound.
- **Personality and Temperament:** Scent hounds hunt with their noses, following scent trails laid down by their quarry. Like his more visually focused cousins, a scent hound on a trail can become obsessed, making that human hollering at him irrelevant for the moment.

Too often, if a dog does what a person wants him to do, he's labeled "intelligent," and if he's not so compliant, he's called "stupid." But think about it: Do intelligent people always do what they're told? The ones I know are more inclined to think things through and make their own decisions. It's no different with dogs, and an intelligent dog is not necessarily easy to train or willing to obey. In fact, intelligence is completely independent from biddability (eagerness to do what we bid, or tell, the dog to do). Some very smart dogs are not very biddable because their ancestors were also bred to think and work independently. Other highly intelligent dogs are extremely biddable because their historical job descriptions required them to work paw in hand with people.

When it comes to training your individual dog, you will find it helpful to understand what his breed (or breeds, if he's a mix) was developed to do. And of course, most important of all, you also need to pay attention to his own individual personality and style.

- **Trainability:** Although they can be trained, hounds aren't as interested in taking human direction as are many other dogs. The big challenge when training any hound is motivation—the dog will ask repeatedly "What's in it for me?"
- **Breed Examples:** Scent hounds include the Basset Hound, Beagle, Bloodhound, Norwegian Elkhound, and Petit Basset Griffon Vendéen.

*The Non-Sporting Group includes the Dalmatian.*

### The Non-Sporting Group

Non-Sporting is a catchall group for breeds that don't seem to fit into other groups, although many of them could easily be included elsewhere. Because there is no particular rationale for placing a breed in the Non-Sporting Group, there is also no particular set of traits that characterize breeds in the group. Some have the energy, work ethic, size, and strength of working and sporting dogs. Others are more like toys or terriers in size and attitude. If your chosen canine is classified as Non-Sporting by the AKC, find out where other registries put his breed for better insights, and of course, research his particular breed.

The Non-Sporting Group includes the American Eskimo Dog, Bichon Frise, Boston Terrier, Bulldog, Chinese Shar-Pei, Chow Chow, Dalmatian, Lhasa Apso, Poodle, and Shiba Inu.

*The Golden Retriever is a member of the Sporting Group.*

## The Sporting Group

- **Original Purpose:** Sporting dogs were developed to work alongside hunters bearing firearms.
- **Size:** Sporting dogs range in size from the small Cocker Spaniel to the tall and rangy setters and the powerfully built retrievers.
- **Personality and Temperament:** Although big differences exist in temperament within the group, in general you can expect sporting dogs to be very trainable, affectionate, and athletic, to have a high pain threshold, and to need lots of exercise. Some are extremely rambunctious, especially when young. Energy and enthusiasm, combined with their high tolerance for discomfort, can make some of the sporting dogs a real handful.
- **Trainability:** Although big differences exist in temperament within the group, in general you can expect sporting dogs to be very trainable.
- **Breed Examples:** The Sporting Group includes some of the most popular breeds for family pets, including retrievers, spaniels, setters, and pointing breeds. Some of the breeds included are the Brittany, Chesapeake Bay Retriever, Cocker Spaniel, English Springer Spaniel, Flat-Coated Retriever, Golden Retriever, Irish Setter, Labrador Retriever, Pointer, and Vizsla.

## The Terrier Group

- **Original Purpose:** The name "terrier" comes from the Latin *terre*, or ground. Terriers, many of whom were developed to hunt or kill game animals and vermin, are bred to "go to ground," or follow tough prey armed with lethal teeth and claws into underground dens.

- **Size:** Terriers range from the small and easily toted breeds to the substantial "king of the terriers," the Airedale.
- **Personality and Temperament:** Terriers are feisty, independent, bold, determined, clever, intense, lively, brave, and intelligent, and they don't always see the point in doing what you tell them. As companions, most terriers are also affectionate and playful. Their high prey drive makes them quick to chase anything that moves, and they tend to bark—I've seen terriers scold their people for making mistakes.
- **Trainability**: Some of the terrier breeds retain more of their hunting instincts than others, and although they are very intelligent, they don't always see the point in following their owners' instructions. They are often said to be hard to train, but the trick to training a terrier is to be patient and to provide motivation. Consistency, patience, and a sense of humor will help you not only survive but enjoy the training process.

*The Bull Terrier belongs to the Terrier Group.*

- **Breed Examples:** Terrier Group breeds include the Airedale Terrier, American Staffordshire Terrier, Border Terrier, Bull Terrier, Cairn Terrier, Kerry Blue Terrier, Miniature Schnauzer, Parson Russell Terrier, Staffordshire Bull Terrier, and West Highland White Terrier.

### The Toy Group

- **Original Purpose:** The breeds of the Toy Group were developed, for the most part, to be full-time companions, small enough to carry around or cuddle on a lap and cute enough to stimulate people's nurturing instincts.
- **Size:** The toy breeds are by definition small, "lap-sized" companions. The group name is unfortunate, though, because despite their small physical stature, these dogs are every bit as intelligent and capable of being trained as are their larger cousins.

*The Toy Group includes the Chihuahua.*

- **Personality and Temperament:** Some of the toys have very terrier-like traits, including a high prey drive and lots of energy. Others still retain some of the "birdiness"—or desire to find, flush, and retrieve game birds—of their sporting forebears.
- **Training:** Too many toy dogs are neglected in terms of training, but make no mistake—these tiny animals are full-fledged dogs, and they can be trained to do nearly anything a big dog can do. Toy dogs can be trained to excel in the show ring and in obedience, agility, rally, tracking, lure coursing, therapy work, and everyday doggy activities. Care must be taken to keep them safe because of their physical vulnerability, but toy dogs are highly trainable and are not wimps. Their small size does make some modifications in training methods necessary in some cases, but their brains and hearts are as big as those of any other dog.
- **Breed Examples:** Toy Group breeds include the Cavalier King Charles Spaniel, Chihuahua, Maltese, Miniature Pinscher, Papillon, Pekingese, Pomeranian, Pug, Shih Tzu, and Yorkshire Terrier.

### The Working Group

- **Original Purpose:** The Working Group includes a diverse group of breeds designed for different types of work. Members of this group have served as guard dogs, hunting companions, messengers, draft animals, herders, livestock guardians—all jobs that require energy, courage, strength, medium to large size, determination, pain tolerance, and problem-solving ability.
- **Size:** Dogs of the Working Group are all large, and the group

includes the heaviest breeds.

- **Personality and Temperament:**
Dogs from the Working Group often
have dominant personalities that will
resist the bully and walk all over the
wimp. These big, strong, energetic dogs
tolerate pain and discomfort well and
can be difficult to manage.

- **Trainability:** Intelligence,
determination, and problem-solving
skills make for superdogs when
directed into acceptable directions, but
without training (as well as exercise and
management), a dog with these traits
can quickly become destructive or even
dangerous. Training must be consistent
and fair to be effective.

- **Breed Examples:** Working Group breeds
include the Akita, Bernese Mountain Dog,
Boxer, Doberman Pinscher, Great Dane,
Mastiff, Newfoundland, Rottweiler, St.
Bernard, and Siberian Husky.

Although all dogs are individuals, their
ancestries determine the range of physical,
mental, and behavioral traits each of them
possesses. Learning about the history and
purpose of your dog's breed (or breeds,
if he has a mixed heritage) will help you understand why he does
some of the things he does and will help you choose the training
tools and methods that will work best for both of you.

*Working Group breeds
include the Bernese
Mountain Dog.*

*Chapter*

# 3

# NURTURE

## *A Healthy Mind in a Healthy Body*

Your dog was born with his own individual mixture of talent and potential. As a domestic animal, he depends on people to help him make the most of his physical and mental assets in the context of "life with people." After all, he's designed to be a dog, and he's very good at that. It's up to you to help him modify and control the traits that are considered "good" in human terms, which may be a challenge for him. Hopefully your dog's dam (his mother) had good care before and during her pregnancy, because the prenatal health of the mother affects the development of her young, in dogs as in people. And hopefully he had equally good care from his birth until the day you brought him home. Now it's your turn to see that he gets the care and training he needs to develop to his fullest potential. Have you ever tried to learn something when you aren't feeling up to par? It isn't easy, is it? It's no different for your dog. The mind is healthier if the body is healthy, and a healthy mind learns more quickly and remembers longer. Good behavior and the ability to learn are profoundly affected by many factors in your dog's life, such as whether he gets plenty of exercise every day, lives in a safe environment, feeds on appropriate amounts of high-quality food, receives proper grooming, and gets good veterinary care. This chapter will show you how to provide your dog with these things, and in doing so, set the stage for effective training.

## EXERCISE

One of the most overlooked requirements for good canine behavior, as well as health and longevity, is regular exercise.

### Benefits of Exercise

A good daily workout will help to control your dog's weight, tone his muscles, build strong bones and maintain the joints, keep his cardiovascular system healthy, and boost his immune system. Exercise will also expend energy and alleviate boredom, two of the

*Healthy, well-cared-for mothers produce healthier puppies.*

leading causes of unwanted behaviors in pet dogs. He will be calmer and less prone to distractions if he gets the exercise he needs. And here's a bonus—keeping your dog in shape will get you up and moving, improving your own physical and emotional health while you strengthen the bond between you and your dog. What more could you ask for?

## How Much Exercise Does Your Dog Need?

Unfortunately, a lot of dogs need a lot more exercise. Some breeds require more physical activity than others, but all healthy dogs need some activity. If you haven't yet chosen your dog, be sure that you know how much and what type of exercise he's going to need. If you already have a dog, you probably have some idea of his energy level by now, but still, understanding his heritage will help you figure out what you need to do to satisfy his need to move.

All dogs require and deserve an investment of human time to be the fine companions they are meant to be. Frankly, if you don't have the time (or desire) to fulfill your dog's exercise needs, then

you either have the wrong breed or individual or the wrong kind of pet for this stage of your life.

## Types of Exercise

So exactly what kind of exercise am I talking about? Do you have to run weekly marathons to please your dog? No, of course not (although I've known a few dogs who probably would think that was the best idea since bagged kibble). On the other hand, you do have to make some effort beyond opening the back door and sending your dog out on his own. (Even if you have more than one dog, unless they are very young, they probably won't get the exercise they need without your direction.) Your dog wants you to throw his ball, take him for walks, and organize "mind games" like hide-and-seek. It's your responsibility—and should be your pleasure—to help him burn energy and bust boredom.

### Basic Obedience

Practicing basic obedience skills will help, and other kinds of training will provide variety. (See Chapters 6, 7, and 8.) The payoff for you will be a better-behaved companion who is much more pleasant to have at your side, whether out and about or relaxing at home.

### Dog Sports

If you enjoy the time you spend one-on-one in training your dog, and if you have the time and resources, you might want to try training in one or more formal dog sports, such as agility. Your dog does not have to be registered or even purebred to participate (more on that in Chapter 10). Nor do you have to limit yourself and your dog to sports he's "supposed to do"—I have done retriever training on land and in the water with my Australian Shepherds, who are bred to tend livestock. As long as you and your dog have fun and your dog's physical traits don't put him at an unsafe disadvantage, why not give some different things a try?

## What Happens if Your Dog Doesn't Exercise

So what happens if your dog doesn't get the exercise he needs? He'll probably get fat and may become depressed. He'll almost

**Size and Energy**

Size and energy level do not necessarily go together. Some small breeds—notably the terriers but also some toys and other smaller dogs—need a lot of exercise. Fortunately, their size lets them run off some of their steam in your house and yard. On the other hand, some large breeds have relatively low exercise needs and are satisfied with two or three reasonable walks a day and an occasional good run. Then again, some big dogs are dynamos! Energy level is another reason it's important to learn about the breed or breeds that make your dog who he is.

*All dogs need exercise, but it's important to understand your dog's limitations. For instance, brachycephalic (short-nosed) dogs like this Boston Terrier are prone to overheating because panting does not cool them as well as it does longer-muzzled dogs.*

certainly be rambunctious, destructive, and hard to handle, and he'll find it almost impossible to focus on whatever training you try to give him.

Your dog will also find ways to entertain himself, and you probably won't like his idea of fun. Bored dogs with too much energy typically like to chase anything that moves, hunt, dig, bark, chew, "landscape" yards, escape, and go looking for adventure. Dog owners tend to call these behaviors "bad," but they are really normal reactions to physical and mental boredom. If we expect our dogs to live within the confines of modern life, then we owe them the time and effort it takes to find safe and suitable outlets for their energy and intelligence.

As your dog matures and loses some of that wild youthful enthusiasm, it may be tempting to skip his exercise. While he may not need as much exercise as he once did to settle him down, throughout his adult life and into old age, as long as he's reasonably healthy, your dog will continue to need and want regular exercise.

## Dealing With Physical Limitations

Health problems can affect your dog's ability to exercise, and if he is younger than two years old, elderly, overweight, or a long-time couch potato, you will want to take some precautions to prevent exercise-related problems or injuries. (You might want to get a checkup yourself if you pick an activity that gets both of you moving.) Regardless of his age, if your dog has physical limitations, ask your vet to help you design a suitable exercise program.

## SAFETY

You are also responsible for your dog's safety. Some precautions are simple. An identification tag on your dog's collar and a tattoo or microchip for permanent identification can bring him home if he's ever lost. Keeping him safely fenced in your yard and on leash when away from home will protect him from many hazards, including vehicles, other animals, and toxic chemicals, among others. And of course, training and socialization will give him the behavioral skills he needs to live with you and others without causing harm or getting into trouble.

Some safety measures are less obvious but equally important when it comes to training and exercising your dog. Let's take a look at some dangers and how you can lessen their threat.

**Did You Know?**

Brachycephalic (short-nosed) breeds are less tolerant of vigorous exercise or hot weather because they cannot cool themselves efficiently.

### Cold

Most dogs tolerate all but the coldest temperatures pretty well, but tiny dogs and those with short coats and little body fat have trouble maintaining normal body temperatures in cold weather. Frostbite, although not common in dogs, can affect areas with less hair, particularly the ears.

#### *Prevention*

A sweater or jacket can help, but whether he's dressed or not, watch your dog for signs of cold (shivering, lifting his paws, asking to be let in), and avoid outdoor jaunts in bad weather if he's not up to it.

### Environmental Hazards

Dogs are even more susceptible to the dangers posed by chemicals in our environment than we are. They are closer to the ground, breathing in all the things we humans put there, and if they walk or swim through "gunk," they lick it off rather than washing up or leaving their shoes at the door.

#### *Prevention*

Be alert to the chemicals in your dog's environment. Does he walk through grass full of pesticides and herbicides? No matter

*Small dogs may benefit from a sweater or jacket in cold weather.*

what the technicians say, lawn and garden chemicals on skin and in respiratory and digestive systems can make for a sick dog. If you walk outdoors in the winter, salt and other ice-melting chemicals stick to your dog's feet and can make him sick. If your dog swims, he may be immersed in chlorine, petroleum products, lawn chemicals, and other potentially hazardous substances. (You also might want to ask your vet about potential parasites from water in your area.) Chemicals used in the house, like carpet powders and some cleaning products, also can cause acute and chronic health problems.

Am I suggesting that you live dirty and never go out? Of course not. But do be aware of the chemicals you use, minimize your dog's exposure, and hand wash them off his body if he becomes exposed.

## Growing Pains

This caution applies specifically to puppies and adolescents who are still growing. Growth occurs in soft areas of immature bone found near the ends of the puppy's leg bones. These areas, the epiphyseal plates or epiphyses, are commonly referred to as growth plates. As the puppy matures, calcium and minerals replace the soft portion of the bone, and most growth stops. The exact age at which the growth plates close varies from about 10 to 18 months, and small dogs stop growing sooner than big dogs.

### Prevention

Open growth plates are vulnerable to fractures and other injuries that can stop growth prematurely and cause permanent damage to the bone, so it's important to monitor the kind of exercise your dog gets while young. The occasional leap probably won't hurt, but repetitive high-impact or leg-twisting activities like jumping over hurdles, weaving through agility poles, or leaping after flying discs have the potential to damage the growth plates or injure the joints and should be postponed until growth has stopped. If you want to be sure, ask your vet to X-ray your puppy to see whether the growth plates are closed, but if you wait until dogs of your breed typically reach their full height, your dog should be good to go.

## Canine Safety

Be sensible about how you exercise your dog. Our dogs can't keep us from doing dumb things, but they can be hurt or killed by our poor judgment. The person at the other end of the leash can be hurt as well. So to keep everyone safe:

- Use a leash. In most cities it is the law, and even if it isn't, a leash can save your dog's life.

- Pay attention to how the weather affects your dog. Be cautious about exercising him outdoors when it's very warm or very cold.

- Don't run your dog alongside your vehicle, whether on or off leash. You're teaching your dog to chase cars—a sport that is usually fatal in the long run—and he could easily be caught under the wheels of your own car. He also could cause an accident.

- Don't ride a bicycle with your dog on a regular leash. It's too easy for the dog to pull you over or to run into the bike. If you want to ride with your dog beside you (and he's big enough, old enough, and healthy enough to join you without hurting growing bones), special devices are available for attaching a dog to a bicycle safely via a strong spring. You can find them through pet supply stores.

- Take your dog in for regular checkups and keep his vaccinations up to date, especially if you take him to places frequented by other dogs who could carry—or catch—diseases or parasites.

- Don't make your dog a "weekend warrior." That's asking for injuries. A little exercise every day is much better than a lot of exercise once in a while.

- Check your dog frequently for lumps, bumps, cuts, and other exercise-related problems, especially on his feet, legs, ears, and eyes.

## Heat

Spring and summer are perfect for playing outdoors with our dogs, but exercising in hot weather can be dangerous. Dogs cool their bodies by panting, which is not a very efficient way to maintain normal body temperature. This can be a problem for any dog in hot weather and more so for those with short muzzles (brachycephalic breeds) and heavy coats. If your dog's body temperature exceeds the normal range (99.5° to 102.8°F [37.5° to 39.3°C]) for even a few minutes, he may suffer permanent brain and organ damage from heatstroke, or die.

### *Prevention*

To prevent heatstroke, never leave your dog in a car in warm weather, even with the windows open. Avoid hard activity during the heat of the day, especially when humidity is high, and be sure that your dog has access to cool water every 20 to 30 minutes. Keep him in the shade as much as possible to keep him from absorbing heat and getting sunburned (yes, dogs sunburn). Avoid paved surfaces, especially blacktop—your dog's body is much closer to their heat than your own, and he is barefoot to boot. Excessive panting; bright red or pale gums; bright red tongue; thick, sticky saliva; rapid panting; vomiting and/or diarrhea; weakness; dizziness; or shock are signs of overheating. If your dog begins to show any of those symptoms, let him rest and cool off in a shady spot. You can help him cool down by wetting his belly and the pads of his feet with cool water.

## Overexertion

Be cautious when starting or upgrading an exercise program for your dog, and always be alert to signs of overexertion—very heavy panting, irregular breathing, stumbling, and appearing to want to slow down or stop.

### *Prevention*

If your dog seems to be tiring, slow down or stop and rest. If you want to jog or run with your dog, be sure that he's up to your pace and duration. Most dogs will faithfully try to keep up with you, and some will become so absorbed in what they're doing that they keep going when they shouldn't. Pushing your dog past his limits, especially in hot weather, could injure or even kill him.

*Swimming can be great exercise for dogs who enjoy it, but the pool should be off-limits for your dog unless a responsible person is there to supervise.*

Don't exercise your dog hard right before or right after he eats, and learn to recognize signs of bloat, especially if your dog is of a breed with a high incidence of that deadly problem. (See box "What You Should Know about Bloat.")

## Road Hazards

Concrete or asphalt can become hot enough in summer to burn your dog's footpads, and repetitive pounding on hard surfaces can damage his joints and contribute to arthritis. In addition, gravel can cut or scrape his pads or even get stuck between the pads and injure his feet.

### Prevention

If you jog, run, or bicycle with your dog, try to keep him on grass, dirt, or other softer surfaces. Special booties are also available to protect the footpads from injury—if you try them, be sure that they fit well and are on securely without being too tight.

## Water Hazards

Many dogs love to swim, and swimming is excellent exercise. Even dogs who have health problems that preclude a lot of weight-bearing exercise benefit from swimming. But many dogs drown every year, making preventive measures crucial to your dog's safety.

### *Prevention*

If you're lucky enough to have a pool, protect your dog as you would a child. Teach him where the steps are, but don't trust him to remember. No matter how good a swimmer he is, don't allow him to have access to the pool without a responsible adult around. Even a strong swimmer can tire, panic, and drown. If you have a pool cover, be absolutely certain that there are no access points where he can slip under and become trapped. Dogs also have been known to fall through pool covers and drown. The same goes for ice—a dog who falls through ice will drown if he can't find the opening or is unable to pull himself out. Supervision is key!

## NUTRITION

Good nutrition—and lack of good nutrition—can profoundly affect health and behavior. The following food-related health problems may result in a dog who not only feels unwell but who exhibits unwanted behaviors.

- **Food Allergies:** Some dogs suffer "hot spots," or raw, itchy sores, as well as diarrhea, vomiting, and other problems due to food allergies or sensitivities. Have you ever tried to focus on learning or minding your manners when you itched all over or

### What You Should Know About Bloat

Bloat (also known as gastric dilatation-volvulus or gastric torsion) is a life-threatening condition that can affect any dog at any age. Dogs with deep chests, like Boxers, Dachshunds, Golden Retrievers, Great Danes, Labrador Retrievers, and Rottweilers, are particularly at risk. Bloat occurs when pressure from a large amount of gas in the stomach causes the stomach to twist, a condition called volvulus or torsion. When torsion occurs, the esophagus is twisted shut and the dog can no longer relieve the pressure by vomiting or belching. As pressure builds, the flow of blood to and from the heart decreases, the heartbeat becomes erratic, the stomach lining begins to die, and toxins build up. The liver, pancreas, spleen, and bowel may be damaged, and the stomach may rupture. The dog suffers terrible pain, goes into shock, and if not treated immediately, dies.

Symptoms of bloat or impending bloat include abdominal distention, retching, salivation, restlessness, refusal to lie down, depression, loss of appetite, lethargy, weakness, or rapid heart rate. If you think that your dog may be bloating, get him to your vet immediately. Call to let the office know that you're on your way with a bloating dog, and drive carefully.

Death from bloat is common even with treatment, so prevention is the best cure. Feed your dog two or three meals a day rather than one, and don't exercise him within two hours of a meal.

had stomach problems? Allergies can be deceptive, too, because they can develop over time—your dog can become allergic to a food he has eaten for a long period without any problems.

- **Obesity:** Obesity is rampant in dogs, and it affects their lives in the same ways it affects human beings, causing or exacerbating heart disease, diabetes, arthritis, and other problems that make for a shorter, more uncomfortable, less fulfilling life. If your dog has inherited the potential for orthopedic problems such as hip or elbow dysplasia, luxating patellas, osteochondrosis, or spinal problems, excess weight will increase the odds that those problems will occur. In short, your dog will live a longer, healthier, happier life if you keep him from getting fat, and he will be a better companion.

- **Other Health Problems:** Some diet-related problems take a long time to appear and may be blamed on other factors. Lack of energy, hyperactivity (meaning chronically out-of-control, unfocused, frantic movement, not normal high energy), chronic urinary or bowel problems, chronic yeast infections, and other health issues are often related to diet.

Fortunately, nutrition is another area of your dog's life in which you have virtually complete control. By learning the basics of nutrition, controlling your dog's food intake, helping him maintain a healthy weight, and feeding him on a schedule, you will improve his health and behavior.

Food Ingredients and Allergies

These common dog food ingredients may cause problems in sensitive or allergic dogs:

- beef
- corn
- dyes
- poultry
- soy
- wheat

## Learn Nutrition Basics

First, learn the basics of sound canine nutrition. The subject is beyond the scope of this book, but good information is available in books and on the Internet. Second, don't rely on promotional hype—read dog food labels, and if you feed the same food for a long time, reread the label occasionally. Manufacturers sometimes change their formulas, and ingredients don't always support claims made for products. (I have seen foods and treats containing corn and wheat—two of the most common allergens—promoted as "good for dogs with allergies.") Remember too that advertising adds to the price of dog foods, and those you see all the time on television and in magazines aren't necessarily the best ones for your dog.

Although the best specific formulation depends on the individual animal, when choosing a dog food, look for high-

*High-quality food in the right amount will keep your dog healthy and set the stage for effective training.*

quality protein, preferably from meat sources; carbohydrates from vegetable sources and few if any grains (preferably no corn or wheat); high-quality fats (again, preferably not from corn); reasonable amounts of vitamins and minerals; and preferably no dyes, fillers, or chemical preservatives.

## Control Your Dog's Food Intake

Control how much your dog eats, and understand that the portions recommended on dog food packages are often a lot more food than the average dog needs. How much you should feed your dog is determined by his activity level, the nutritional quality and digestibility of the food he eats, his age, his general health, and his individual metabolism. Use the recommended portion as a starting point, and adjust the amount according to how your individual dog does on the food. Use a standard measuring tool to dish up his food—make sure that the "cup" you use as a scoop isn't closer to two cups. And don't forget to include treats in his daily caloric intake! Limit high-calorie treats, and try some healthful, low-cal goodies—I often use bits of raw carrot and green beans for training treats to keep the calories under control.

## Keep Your Dog at a Healthy Weight

Oddly enough, most people I speak to whose dogs are too fat blame everything except the most common cause—too much food. Granted, lack of exercise is often linked to obesity as well, and in very rare cases, metabolic disease may be a factor. But most people overestimate both how much food their dogs need and how much exercise their dogs get. The bottom line is that fat dogs are tubby because they eat more calories than they burn. And since most modern dogs are not in charge of their own diets or exercise regimes, guess who's to blame?

I know, I know, your dog uses those big "I'm so hungry" eyes like daggers to your heart, and he gobbles whatever you offer. If you think about the life of a wild canid, you'll see the logic of this instinct to eat, eat, eat. When there's no big bag of dog food in the pantry, it makes perfect survival sense to eat when you can because you may not catch your next meal for a day or two. But when regular meals plus treats and goodies replace the unpredictable wild menu, uncontrolled eating makes for a chubby pooch. So what's a dog owner to do?

### Decrease Food, Increase Exercise

Your dog isn't going to put himself on a diet, so if he needs to trim down, you have to help him. The obvious first step is to cut back on the amount of food he gets per meal and per day. If possible, increase your dog's activity level (but build up slowly, especially if he's considerably overweight and has been a couch potato). Most dogs will pretend their bellies are empty even if they've just filled them, but if you honestly think that your dog is still hungry after eating his regular food, here are a few tricks to fill

*Offer treats in moderation.*

him without fattening him:

1. If you feed dry dog food, soak a quarter of the meal in water for about half an hour. The soaked pieces will expand and be more filling. At mealtime, mix half his regular dry portion with the soaked food—you'll cut the calories by a fourth, but your dog won't know he's getting less food.

2. Supplement your pooch's regular grub with low-calorie, high-fiber foods—unsalted green beans (raw fresh beans are great), whole or sliced raw carrot (my dogs line up at the refrigerator every morning for their whole carrots), lettuce or spinach, plain canned pumpkin (not pie filling), or unsalted, air-popped popcorn (unless he's allergic to corn). If your dog has never had veggies, he may think you've lost your mind at first, but trust me, most dogs soon discover that this is good stuff—and fun to crunch.

If these tactics don't work, ask your vet about a weight-loss or lower-calorie food—but keep in mind that many dogs remain fat for years while eating too much low-cal food. Most would be better off with smaller amounts of a good maintenance food.

### *Monitor Weight and Condition*

Monitor your dog's weight and condition throughout his life, and adjust what he gets accordingly. He will need less food as an adult than he did as a puppy and adolescent, and he may need even less as he ages. Weigh your dog every few months, and evaluate how he looks and acts. (See box "Is Your Dog Fat?") A healthy dog is neither too thin nor too fat. He has a shiny coat, healthy skin, and clear eyes. He should not have bad breath or excess gas. Excess or insufficient weight, unexplained changes in weight or eating habits, lack of energy, unhealthy skin or coat, or sudden unexplained changes in behavior can be signs of health problems that warrant a trip to your vet.

### Is Your Dog Fat?

With all due respect to your veterinarian, don't rely on her to tell you if your dog is too fat. Most vets are so used to seeing overweight pets and so rarely see dogs in truly fit condition that unless the dog's belly is dusting the floor, they don't say much. So it's up to you to keep your dog at his healthiest weight.

Place your index finger and thumb on opposite sides of the ridge of your dog's spine near his shoulders, and run your fingers down his spine toward his tail. You should feel his ribs without pressing down. You also should see a definite "waist," or narrowing behind his ribs, when you look down on him when he's standing.

## Follow a Feeding Schedule

When and how you feed your dog are also important and have even more obvious connections to training and behavior than overall nutrition does. I do not recommend free feeding—giving your dog access to food all the time. Contrary to a widespread notion that free-fed dogs won't overeat, many dogs with free access to grub eat themselves to blimphood. (When my Australian Shepherd, Jay, came to me at four years old, he had been free fed and weighed 83 pounds [37.6 kg]. He was so fat that he couldn't roll over. He now weighs a healthy 53 pounds [24.0 kg], and although he might think he'd like to eat all day, he's much healthier and happier now.)

Scheduled meals not only keep most dogs at a healthier weight, they also make it easier for you to monitor your pet's health. The first sign of illness is often loss of interest in food, which you may not notice right away if your dog is free fed. On a practical level, if you travel with your dog or if you board him while you're away, he'll almost certainly be fed on a schedule, and the change will add more stress to the experience. Leaving food out all the time may also attract animals and insects into your home.

Putting yourself in control of your dog's access to food facilitates training in several ways. As we saw in Chapter 2, in a pack, the alpha essentially controls the resources, so reminding your dog at every meal that you control his food reinforces his subordinate social status in concrete terms. Regular meals make housetraining easier because food that goes in on schedule comes out on schedule. Finally, if you use treats to motivate your dog when you train, he will be much more interested in them if he doesn't think of food as something he can get whenever he wants, without working for it.

## GROOMING

What does grooming have to do with training and behavior, you ask? Several things, actually. If you approach grooming not as a chore but as intimate one-on-one time you share with your dog, grooming sessions become an integral part of your relationship. And in training, your relationship with your dog is critical. If you're gentle (as you should be—who likes to have his hair pulled or paws squeezed?), your dog learns to trust you and your hands, and trust is critical in training. Regular grooming sessions also keep your dog (and your house) cleaner and give you a chance to check for cuts, bites, bumps, sore spots, uninvited parasites, and other early signs of health problems.

## Coat Care

Your dog's coat is the most obvious grooming project. Long coats need to be brushed several times a week to remove loose hair and to prevent tangles from turning into mats that can retain moisture, dirt, debris, and even live pests, leading to itching, pain, and even open sores and infections. Short coats benefit from regular brushing, too, because it removes dirt and loose hair and distributes oils that lubricate the skin and hair. Some breeds must be trimmed, clipped, or hand-stripped (a process of pulling out the dead hairs) from time to time. Some dogs also need to be bathed regularly, while others need only an infrequent bath. Whatever he requires, keeping your dog clean will make him a healthier, more pleasant, and more trainable companion and will help to keep your housekeeping chores to a minimum.

*Regular grooming will make your dog a healthier, more pleasant companion.*

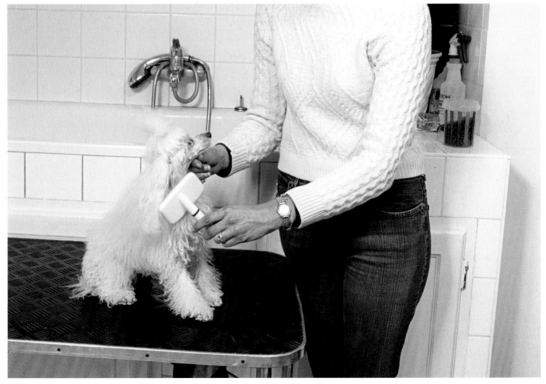

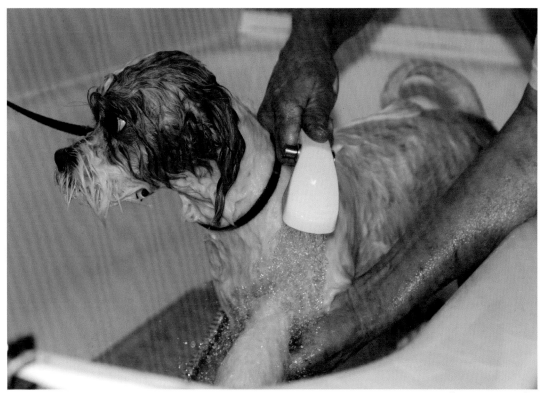

*Your dog requires regular brushing and bathing to look and feel his best.*

### How to Do It

Grooming methods and tools vary from breed to breed and from coat type to coat type. In general, coats should be brushed or combed from the skin to the outer ends of the hairs to remove dirt and debris, prevent tangles and mats, and distribute oils. We could devote a whole book to describing how to groom all breeds of dogs, so your best bet is to check your library for books about your specific breed (or something close to what your dog looks like, if he's a mixed breed) or speak to a breeder or a knowledgeable groomer.

Bathing most dogs is not difficult, and most of them get used to being bathed even if they don't like it much. Here are a few things you can do to simplify the process:

1. Assemble all your supplies before you begin: a mild shampoo formulated for dogs; towels; a shower attachment or unbreakable container for rinsing; leash for controlling your wet dog after the bath.
2. If your dog has long hair, brush it thoroughly and remove all

loose hair, tangles, and mats before you wet him.

3. Carefully put your dog into the tub (the kitchen sink will work if he's small). You might want to place a rubber mat or a towel on the bottom to give him better footing.

4. Wet your dog with lukewarm water.

5. Apply dog shampoo, following the instructions on the bottle. Begin with a "collar" of suds around the neck just behind the ears to prevent any fleas from hiding in his ears. Be very careful not to get shampoo in his eyes—it can burn them. Also, keep water and shampoo out of his ears, where they may promote infections.

6. Gently massage shampoo into your dog's fur. Use a clean washcloth to clean his face and head.

7. Rinse thoroughly. Be sure to check the sneaky places where suds tend to hide, like the armpits, groin, under the tail, and the groove of the belly beneath the ribs.

8. Towel as much moisture out of the fur as possible. If your dog has long hair, press and squeeze the water from the coat into the towel—rubbing will create tangles.

9. If your dog has a long coat, gently comb or brush the damp hair into place.

10. If you wish, blow your dog's coat dry with a dryer set on "cool"—hot air can dry his skin and can cause your dog to overheat if the drying process takes more than a minute or two.

11. Keep your dog out of drafts until he's completely dry. You'll probably want to confine him to a crate or a room with a washable floor until he's dry.

12. Most dogs need to potty after a bath—take your dog out on a leash to keep him from rolling his nice clean coat in the dirt.

Reward your dog at various stages of the bathing process, and be gentle. If you make the experience as pleasant as possible, the next bath will be easier for both of you.

## Dental Care

Poor dental health can cause behavioral issues (especially "illegal" chewing) and lack of focus and can contribute to other serious health problems, including the proliferation of bacteria that can cause life-threatening damage to the heart and other organs. Unhealthy teeth and gums also cause "dog breath," a barrier to close dog–human relations and a mostly preventable problem. So

for both your sakes, set up a regular dental care program for your dog, including at-home care and regular veterinary care.

### How to Do It

Have your vet show you the right dental care products for your dog and teach you to use them. Ideally, your dog should have his teeth brushed every day, but realistically, brushing several times a week (with canine toothpaste, not the human kind, which will make him sick) will help to keep his teeth and gums clean and healthy and give you an opportunity to check his mouth for injuries, soreness, or growths.

Dental checkups also should be part of your dog's regular veterinary exams, as should thorough periodic cleaning and polishing under anesthesia, usually once or twice a year. Feeding your dog a high-quality dry dog food and providing him with safe chew toys, like Nylabones, can help to keep his teeth clean as well.

*Brushing your dog's teeth will help to keep his teeth and gums clean.*

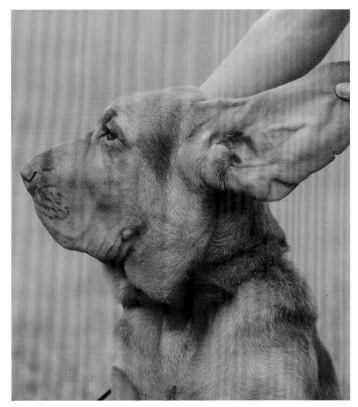

*Inspect your dog's ears at least once a week.*

## Ear Care

Irritations and infections of the ears are very common in dogs. Allergies, hormonal problems, and excess moisture all can promote abnormal growth of yeast or bacteria in the ear canal. Ear mites sometimes take up residence, and if they exist in large numbers or if your dog is sensitive to mite saliva, they'll cause severe itching that can lead to painful secondary infections from scratching. Active dogs also sometimes get water, dirt, plant matter, or other foreign objects in their ears, which can cause problems. Painful or itchy ears are not only a health issue—they are also a training and behavioral issue. No one focuses well with an earache.

### *How to Do It*

Check your dog's ears at least once a week. The skin inside his ear should not look red or inflamed, and you shouldn't see excessive or dirty-looking discharge or smell any strong or unpleasant odors. Even if you don't see anything, if your dog scratches or rubs his head a lot, shakes it, holds it tilted, or doesn't want to have his ears or head touched, something is wrong.

Don't try to treat an ear problem on your own—you can cause more serious damage and delay proper treatment, letting your dog suffer longer and potentially leading to permanent hearing loss. See your vet for treatment, and ask for advice on proper routine ear care for your individual dog.

## Eye Care

Your dog's eyes also may require care. Some breeds are prone to buildup of "eye gunk" at the inner corners of the eyes. This protein-rich discharge can harbor bacteria and lead to infection. It also can stain light-colored hair. And besides, it looks unsightly.

### How to Do It

Gently wipe off eye discharge with a warm, moist towel or tissue. If you see signs of redness, swelling, excess tearing, or discharge, or if your dog squints or paws at his face, see your vet—these can be signs of infection, abrasion, or other problems that can cause permanent damage to the eye. Many breeds are also prone to inherited eye problems, so do your homework and know what to watch for. If you participate in active sports with your dog, consider having his eyes checked every year or two by a canine ophthalmologist using the Canine Eye Registration Foundation (CERF) protocols (and let your dog's breeder know the results).

You also can minimize the risk that your dog will suffer a serious eye injury. First, no matter how much he likes to feel his ears flapping in the wind, he is much safer if he doesn't hang his head out the car window. A speck of dirt or a tiny insect can cause serious damage if it hits soft eye tissue at the speed of a moving vehicle. Chemicals also can damage eyes, so be careful when using shampoo or other substances around your dog's head. Keep his eyes healthy so that he can see your hand signals and tennis balls!

*Foot and nail care are essential parts of the grooming process.*

## Nail and Foot Care

Nail and foot care are absolutely essential—how do you like to walk around with sore feet or ill-fitting shoes? Letting your dog's nails grow so long that they hit the ground is like making him wear bad shoes— ouch! Severely overgrown nails can even curve around and dig into the footpad.

Most dogs need their nails trimmed every two to three weeks. If you don't know how to trim doggy nails, ask (or pay) your vet or a groomer to teach you. Make sure that your clippers are sharp and in good working order so that they don't pinch or pull instead of cutting cleanly.

### How to Do It

The nails should be short enough not to touch the ground, but try not to cut into the quick, the living part of the nail. If your dog's nails are light colored, the quick will look pink from the blood vessels inside it, and you can cut just beyond the quick. Dark nails are more challenging, but if you cut below the spot where the nail narrows and curves downward, you should miss the quick. Trim, then check the end of the nail. If you see a black dot near the center, you're close to the quick. If not, take a little more off and check again. If your dog has dewclaws, the little toes on the insides of the legs above the front feet, don't forget to trim them, too.

If you cut a nail too short and draw blood, don't panic! Put a little styptic powder (available from drug stores) or cornstarch in the palm of your hand and dip the nail in it to stop the bleeding. Then reassure your dog, and be more careful next time.

## HEALTH CARE

Good health care at home and from your veterinarian makes sense for a lot of reasons. For our purposes in this book, it's important to realize that disease and injury have a negative effect on your dog's behavior and his ability to learn new things. How well do you do when you're sick or in pain? Fortunately, you can protect your dog against many threats to his health. We don't have room here for a thorough discussion of canine health care, but I will touch on some of the most important steps you and your vet can take to help your furry training partner live a longer, healthier life.

## Find a Great Vet

Your veterinarian, like your physician, should obviously be someone whose competence you trust. Not so obviously, your veterinarian should also listen to your concerns, answer your questions, and trust you as an important source of information about your dog's health. It's worth the time it takes to find a veterinarian with whom you feel comfortable. After all, you're trusting her with your dog's very life.

So how can you find a great vet? Word of mouth is often the best way. Ask for references from your family, friends, neighbors, and if relevant, your dog's breeder or rescuer. Ask what they like and don't like about their vets and the practices in which they work. You also might check the Internet and the telephone book

*Regular veterinary care will help your dog lead a longer, healthier, happier life.*

55

for listings. Visit the practice, and if possible, meet the vet before you need her. Ask about the things that concern you: hours, emergency provisions, billing procedures, and so on. If you have a dog with special needs, perhaps a specific medical condition or a breed-related issue concerning health care, ask whether the vet has experience in that area. (For instance, sight hounds tend to be sensitive to anesthesia, so you would want a vet who knows that, and ideally, who has experience working with sight hounds.) Overall, be sure that you and your vet are in agreement about your general approach to your dog's care.

Even if you respect and trust your vet (if you don't, find another!), be proactive about your dog's care. Vets tend to be very busy, and even the best vet may not know all there is to know about your breed's particular health issues or your dog's individual history. You and your veterinarian should consider one another partners in your dog's health care.

*Vaccinating your dog is one of the best ways to protect him against disease.*

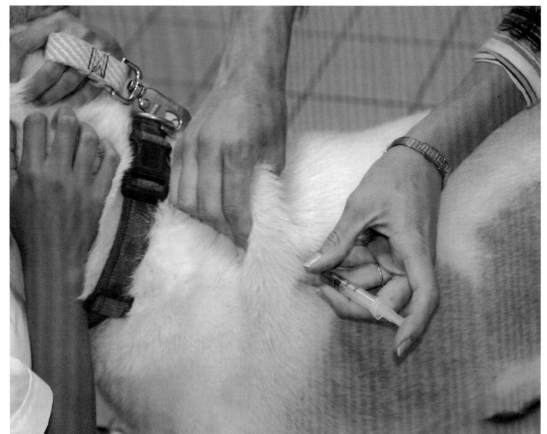

### Drug Sensitivities

We all know someone who is unable to take certain medications because of adverse reactions. It's important to be aware that dogs of some breeds are sensitive to specific drugs or families of drugs, experiencing reactions varying from mild to fatal. Many dogs of the Collie breeds (Collie, Shetland Sheepdog, Australian Shepherd, Border Collie, and mixes of those breeds), for instance, are sensitive to ivermectin, the active ingredient in some medications used to prevent or treat heartworm, mange, and some other parasites. Sight hounds and some other breeds tend to be sensitive to drugs used for anesthesia. Research your dog's breed or breeds, and if you find that your dog is potentially sensitive to a drug, be sure that your veterinarian is aware of the risk. Don't depend on your vet to know—it's nearly impossible to know all the ins and outs of hundreds of breeds of dogs! Your dog's well-being is largely in your hands.

## Vaccinate Your Dog

Vaccinations are a topic of considerable controversy among dog people these days. One view is that of the traditionalists, who believe that puppy vaccinations followed by annual boosters are the way to go. On the other hand, a growing number of veterinarians and dog owners believe that overvaccinating actually damages the animal's immune system, causing a host of chronic health problems. And of course, some people are on the fence, using various vaccination schedules in an attempt to guard against disease without compromising the dog's natural immune system.

Despite the risks, vaccination remains the best ways to protect your dog against some common, highly contagious, deadly diseases, especially during puppyhood. The best thing you can do is educate yourself and speak to your veterinarian about which vaccines your dog needs, and when. If you don't agree with one vet's approach, find another vet.

Disease is easily spread among canines, and vaccination is particularly important if your dog will frequent places where many dogs congregate, including training classes, parks, and possibly canine competitive events. Ask your vet which vaccines are essential where you live or travel with your dog, and ask her advice before taking your puppy out in public if he hasn't finished his puppy shots.

## Keep Your Dog Parasite-Free

In addition to diseases caused by bacteria and viruses, dogs are subject to attack by a variety of parasites, creatures that live on or in the bodies of other animals. Among the most common parasites of dogs are fleas, ticks, mites, intestinal parasites, and heartworms. Parasites spread from one animal to another in a variety of ways, and your dog does not require direct contact with an infected animal to acquire parasites. Although some are merely disgusting, many parasites cause damage directly or carry deadly and debilitating diseases. Parasite prevention and treatment are important throughout your dog's life, so speak to your vet about recommendations for your area.

## Consider Alternative Therapies

Many dog owners have become interested in recent years in health care that transcends traditional veterinary medicine. As in human health care, animal medicine now includes alternative,

*The effort you make to nurture your dog with good grooming, nutrition, health care, exercise, safety precautions, and training will pay off with a healthier, better-behaved canine companion.*

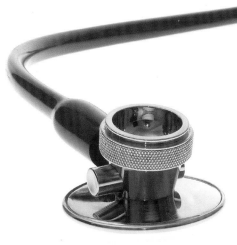

*Alternative therapies consider emotional and physical factors.*

complementary, or holistic practices that consider emotional as well as physical factors in health and illness. The field of nonconventional health care is enormous and includes competent, caring practitioners with formal training and the ability to help where conventional medicine has not. Unfortunately, there are also some dishonest people out there. Some will damage only your bank balance, but some could hurt your dog or delay more effective treatment, so be cautious. That said, many dog owners, including serious competitors in canine athletics, use the formal disciplines of chiropractic, acupuncture, homeopathy, herbal therapy, nutrition, and other practices such as massage therapy, shiatsu, Reiki, TTouch, Contact Reflex, and so forth to treat problems and maintain optimum health and well-being.

So there you have them: exercise, safety, nutrition, grooming, and health care. These are five aspects of your dog's life that can profoundly affect his behavior, his ability to learn and be trained, and ultimately, his relationship with you and the rest of the world. If you take care of these aspects of your dog's life, you will both be happier in the long run, and you will set the stage for more effective training.

# 4

## TRAINING TOOLS

**H**ave you ever tried to use a huge screwdriver to replace the teensy little screw in the hinge of your glasses? Or to pound a nail into a board? How about painting your house with an artist's brush? Or maybe using a hacksaw to slice bread? Silly, right? And not very effective. We all know that the right equipment is important to doing any job well. The same goes for dog training.

### THE RIGHT TOOL FOR THE JOB

The hard part is figuring out just what the right equipment is for you and your dog. And while your choice of screwdriver, paintbrush, or bread knife may be pretty straightforward, your choices for your dog are a bit more complicated.

For one thing, your dog's size, age, physical condition, level of training, and general behavior are all important factors to consider. The size, strength, and experience of the person training the dog also may be important—a healthy 180-pound (81.6-kg) adult man may be able to control an 80-pound (36.3-kg) adolescent dog with one type of collar, whereas his 110-pound (49.9-kg) wife may need more mechanical advantage to avoid being hauled down the street.

Another consideration is the distinction between physical effectiveness and training effectiveness. Some so-called training tools provide control, but they don't enhance learning because they rely on fear and force to prevent certain behaviors without teaching the dog what he's supposed to do. That may make for what seems to be a short-term fix, but brutal methods of control usually lead to more serious problems and certainly damage the relationship between dog and person. Besides, who wants to bully and hurt their best friend?

In the end, the best training tools are those that enhance your ability to communicate clearly with your dog at a particular time. You already have some of these tools; others you may have to buy. You may even find yourself getting rid of some equipment you have tried in the past. Over his lifetime, you'll spend a great deal of money on your dog—don't begrudge yourself a tiny fraction of that amount for the right training tools.

# DOG TRAINING TOOLS YOU ALREADY HAVE

When we think of "tools" for dog training, we usually think of the things we buy, including leashes, collars, whistles, clickers, toys, treats, crates, and so forth. But you already have the three most important tools for training, the tools that determine how your dog perceives you and responds to you: your attitude and actions, your voice, and your body language.

## Attitude and Actions

*Keep a happy, enthusiastic attitude toward training, and your dog will respond in kind.*

Imagine you are trying to learn to live in a foreign culture completely different from your own. You take a total-immersion course—you live with your teacher and rely on your teacher to fill all your needs and desires. You have to learn a whole new language, and you have to learn what behavior is considered polite, what is rude, and what will get you thrown in jail, or worse.

Now imagine Teacher #1. She is very nice to you as long as you make no mistakes. But how can you make no mistakes? You don't understand what she says, and you don't know how to act. When you don't understand, she talks louder. You try to tell her you're not deaf or stupid, you just don't understand, but she doesn't understand you any better than you understand her. You do your best, but you make mistakes. When you do, you never know how

your teacher will react—sometimes she yells, shoves you out in the backyard, maybe even smacks you. Scary stuff! But sometimes she doesn't seem to care. So were you right or wrong?

Contrast that scenario with Teacher #2. She spends time teaching you what to do, and she helps you be correct. When you make a mistake, she calmly shows you the right way, and she rewards you for learning. There are rules, and this teacher reinforces them consistently. She never yells, hits you, or frightens you.

I don't know about you, but I would much prefer to learn from Teacher #2—and so would your dog. Keep in mind that your dog is learning to live not just in a foreign culture but with members of another species. He's learning to understand directions given not just in a foreign language but in an alien form of communication—speech. It's your job to make the difficult job of learning as easy and pleasant as possible for both of you.

*Because dogs are attentive to body language in humans, it's important to stand up straight and convey a sense of confidence to your dog.*

## Voice: How Your Dog Hears You

Most dogs hear exceptionally well, and yet how often have you heard people yell "SIT, FLUFFY!" or "ROCKY, STAY!"? Yelling at a dog who doesn't obey, especially one who doesn't understand the command regardless of volume, strikes me as rather like talking louder to make someone who speaks another language understand. Honestly, if I were plunked down in the middle of Prague, people could holler in Czech until they turned blue and I still wouldn't know what they were saying. The same goes for dogs, no matter what language you speak. I won't give you many hard and fast rules, but here's one: Don't yell at your dog.

Your voice can be used to inspire your dog, too. Dogs tend to like high-pitched happy voices, and they are more inclined to pay attention to people who talk to them with joy in their voices. Experiment as you talk to your dog, and find the voice that makes him wag his tail, prick up his ears, and cock his head at you.

## Body Language

Dogs are very attentive to body language in other animals, including us. If you stand up straight, move confidently, and make any signals you use clear and consistent, your dog will believe that you know what you want and will be more interested in responding to you. If, on the other hand, you seem tentative or threatening, or you stomp, flap your arms, or do other weird things with your body, you'll make your dog as confused as he thinks you are! Even experienced trainers sometimes make movements they don't realize they're making until someone points them out, and those movements can confuse our dogs. So pay attention to not only what you say and how you say it, but consider what you're doing with your posture, arms, legs, head, and face. Have someone watch you work with your dog from time to time to see if you're sending signals you don't realize you're sending.

*Baby gates are helpful for confining dogs to certain parts of the house.*

## TRAINING EQUIPMENT

You don't have to spend a fortune on fancy dog training equipment, but you do need a few things. Let's take a look.

## Baby Gates

Baby gates are useful for restricting your dog's access to certain areas of your house, which is essential when you are teaching house manners and helpful at other times. Although gates won't hold all dogs, most can be taught to respect the boundary even if they can hop over it.

### Types of Gates

Regular pressure-fitted gates are inexpensive and are available from many sources, including home centers, discount stores, baby stores, and pet supply stores. Special extra-tall gates are also available, as are gates for wide openings and wall-mounted gates that swing open.

### Gate Cautions

When using a pressure-fitted gate, be sure that it fits tightly into the door frame so that it won't fall easily. It's a good idea to place the pressure bar on the side of the doorway away from your dog to keep him from catching a leg between the bar and the gate. Also, check your gates periodically for damage—metal parts can become bent and wood can be broken, creating sharp edges. The webbing on the gate itself also can become damaged and potentially dangerous. And of course, be careful when stepping over a gate— I've tripped myself more than once.

## Collars, Harnesses, and Head Halters

Your dog needs at least one collar, probably two, and possibly three or more. Now, I'm not talking about a rhinestone number for fancy dress. I'm talking about collars that your dog wears for different purposes.

If you ask a group of experienced dog trainers about collars, you'll get a wide range of opinions about which ones work well, which ones are dangerous, which ones are ineffective, and which should be outlawed. Because people's opinions are usually based on their own experiences, it may be important to understand the training background of anyone giving you advice. For instance, someone who has never had a dog who weighed more than 25 pounds (11.3 kg) may be violently opposed to the use of a certain type of collar, while someone with a rambunctious 90-pound (40.8-kg) adolescent retriever may consider that collar

**Training Equipment**

The following is a list of equipment you'll need to train your dog:

- collar
- crate
- gate
- leash
- toys
- treats

indispensable. All of which can, of course, be very confusing if you're new to training. In the end, you should weigh the advice you get from people and books, as well as weigh the effectiveness of each collar you try for you and your dog. I use different collars on my dogs depending on the dog's age, level of training, individual personality, and type of activity. You may want to make changes from time to time as well.

Several types of collars are commonly used for basic and more advanced training.

### Flat Collar

***Description and Use:*** A flat or buckle collar is a strip of leather, nylon, or fabric fastened with a buckle or a quick-release clasp. A flat collar or martingale collar (See section "Martingale Collar") are the collars that should carry your dog's name, license, and rabies tags, and they are the only types of collars that your dog should ever wear in his crate or when you are not present. A flat collar should fit so that you can slip two fingers between the collar and your dog's neck, and you should check the fit periodically, especially if you have a growing puppy.

*Check your dog's collar regularly to be sure that it fits properly (especially while he's growing) and is in good repair.*

If you decide to try "clicker training"—a form of positive reinforcement based on operant conditioning (see Chapter 5)—with your dog, you'll probably use a flat collar for training. If you train with a flat collar, you'll need two of them: one free of tags for training and another with tags for regular wear.

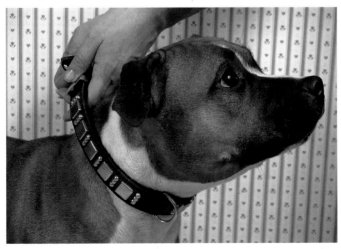

***Advantages:*** A properly fitted flat collar is relatively gentle on the dog's neck. For that reason, this is the only collar that should be used on a young puppy. (A harness may be safer for a very young or small puppy.)

*Disadvantages:* Flat collars provide very little control, and some dogs learn to slip out of them.

### Martingale Collar

*Description and Use:* A martingale collar looks a lot like a flat collar but is made of two pieces: a flat piece that encircles part of the dog's neck and a loop that links the two ends of the flat piece. A martingale collar does not open and must be slipped over your dog's head. The ring to which you attach your leash is attached to the loop portion of the collar, and when the dog pulls against the leash, the loop tightens the flat portion of the collar around the neck. This is particularly useful to prevent collars from slipping off dogs with long, narrow heads and those who have learned to "duck and slip" out of a flat collar. A properly adjusted martingale collar tightens only so far and cannot strangle the dog. Martingales collars are commonly used in agility, flyball, and some other dog sports.

*Your dog should have his identification, license, and rabies tags securely attached to a flat collar that he wears most of the time.*

*Advantages:* The collar cannot strangle the dog if it fits properly, and dogs cannot slip out of martingale collars like they can flat collars.

*Disadvantages:* Like the flat collar, the martingale collar doesn't provide very much control if a dog is big and rambunctious.

### Harnesses

*Description and Use:* A harness usually has two straps linked together. One strap fits around the dog's neck, the other around his body, and the shoulder takes any pulling pressure put on the dog. Harnesses provide very little control

## Other Collars Debunked

Many pet supply stores and other merchants carry collars that can cause severe physical and psychological pain and damage to dogs. I provide the following descriptions in the interest of complete information, and *do not* recommend the use of these collars for most people or dogs. Positive reinforcement is a much more effective and humane way to teach our best friends what we want them to do.

### Choke Collars

**Description and Use:** The choke collar (also called a choke chain, slip chain, slip collar, or sometimes simply training collar) is usually made of metal links, although choke collars are also available in nylon, fabric, and leather. Traditionally, choke collars were the "weapon of choice" in an old-fashioned style of dog training often referred to as "pop and jerk" because it relied on jerking the leash to punish the dog for doing something incorrectly. Because punishment is unfair and a far less effective training method than rewards, knowledgeable dog trainers no longer rely on abusive popping and jerking. Perhaps because of its long and easy availability, this seems to be the collar that most people show up with at beginning obedience classes. The collars often do not fit their dogs and are put on incorrectly.

Choke chains should never be used by an inexperienced dog trainer and should never be used on a puppy.

**Why Some Professionals Use Them:** Used *correctly*, the choke chain can be effective for some training for some dogs—but again, most people use choke chains incorrectly.

**Why You Shouldn't Use Them:** Although many good dog trainers use choke collars without being cruel to their dogs, most people use these collars incorrectly. At best, a choke collar used incorrectly is ineffective. Many dogs learn to ignore the collar—these are the dogs you see gagging and strangling as they drag their people down the street, collar pulled tight as a noose around the dogs' necks. In addition, a collar that fits poorly and is put on wrong has virtually no value as a training tool and gives little control. At its worst, a choke collar can permanently injure your dog's throat and the delicate organs inside.

### Prong Collars

**Description and Use:** A prong (or pinch) collar is made of linked metal segments with prongs that lie along the neck when the collar is slack and that apply pressure around the dog's neck when the collar is tightened by the leash. (The tips of the prongs do not push straight into the dog's neck.)

**Why Some Professionals Use Them:** A prong collar provides control without yanking. In fact, a prong collar should never be yanked. Some professional trainers use this collar when trying to walk or train a large, strong, rambunctious dog who lacks focused attention on his handler. For training, especially at advanced levels of obedience, the prong collar allows for very subtle communication with the dog through minor changes in tightness. The links also can be turned around so that the dog feels no prongs, a few prongs, or all the prongs.

**Why You Shouldn't Use Them:** Used incorrectly, a prong collar is very harsh and can frighten a dog and cause physical pain.

### Electronic Collars

**Description and Use:** Electronic collars, or shock collars, use sound and/or electrical stimulation (shocks) to correct or reinforce behavior. The trainer uses a remote control to operate the collar, which delivers anything from a beep that the dog has been taught to understand (like the click of a clicker—see Chapter 5), to a mild tingle, to a painful shock.

**Why Some Professionals Use Them:** Used correctly by an experienced trainer with good timing, and without causing pain, an electronic collar can be an effective training tool. The use of sounds from the collar's receiver to reinforce correct behaviors and to signal mistakes is especially useful when working a dog at a distance.

**Why You Shouldn't Use Them:** Electrical shocks are often used to punish the dog for doing what he shouldn't do without teaching him what he should do. Think about it: Would you use electrical shocks to teach your children how to behave properly? Shock collars should *never* be used on an aggressive or fearful dog.

for large dogs but may be useful for tiny dogs and puppies, and they may be the only option for a dog with a neck problem. Special harnesses are also used in place of collars for tracking (following a scent trail) and for pulling sports such as weight pulling, carting, mushing (sledding), and so forth.

*Advantages:* The biggest advantage of a harness is that there is no risk of injuring your dog's throat or neck vertebrae. This can be an important consideration for small dogs, especially.

*Disadvantages:* A harness gives very little control. In addition, if you ever plan to participate in any dog sports other than tracking or pulling events, you will need to switch to a collar at some point.

### Head Halters

*Description and Use:* A halter (or head collar) fits over the dog's head, with a strap across the muzzle and another behind the ears, something like a horse's halter. Halters are sold under several names. The designs vary slightly, but they all work on the same basic principle.

*Advantages:* If you control your dog's head, you control your dog, and halters give lots of head control. Used in conjunction with positive training methods, a halter can be a good training tool.

*Disadvantages:* Unfortunately, it's all too easy to rely on the halter and neglect the training. That's okay if the only time you want your dog to listen to you is when you're connected by a halter and leash. But if you want your dog to listen and obey even when he's not wearing a halter, you have to put in the time and effort to train him. There is also some evidence linking use of head halters to injuries to the cervical (neck) vertebrae caused by pulling the head too hard to the side and back, which can easily happen if a rambunctious dog lunges and is stopped short by the halter or if a handler yanks on the leash attached to the collar and essentially gives the dog whiplash.

### Crate

Some people still shy away from using a crate, thinking it

*A harness may work well for a small dog, like this mixed breed, or for a dog with neck or spine problems, but for a large, healthy dog, a harness offers little control.*

cruel. Often this view is based on seeing the crate through human, rather than canine, eyes. Most of us don't like to be confined to a small space or to have our freedom curtailed. Most dogs, though, like their crates—the cozy space is like a den, safe and secure, and many dogs will choose to lie inside their crates even when the doors are open. Crates can be misused, of course, but used properly, a crate is an extremely useful bit of equipment. It will keep your dog from hurting himself or damaging your property when you can't watch him, and it will help to curtail problem behaviors until he is fully trained.

There are other good reasons to crate train your puppy in addition to the safety and mischief issues. If he will travel with you, he'll be safer in a crate rather than loose in a vehicle and will have a familiar home-away-from-home in motel rooms or the in-laws' house. In addition, if your dog ever needs to be confined because of injury or illness, the familiarity of his crate will reduce his stress. All in all, crate training is a good thing for most dogs.

### Types of Crates

Crates come in a wide range of sizes and a multitude of styles, including wire, wood, plastic, aluminum, fabric, and even wicker, and are available from many discount stores as well as pet-supply stores and on-line vendors. If your pup has a long or double coat, he may be more comfortable in a well-ventilated wire crate than in a plastic crate, although if the crate is in your air-conditioned house it won't make much difference. Small dogs and dogs with short coats often prefer the warmer den-like plastic crate. Fabric crates are very popular with canine sports enthusiasts because of their lighter weight, but I wouldn't trust a puppy to a fabric or wicker crate—too easy to chew or even roll over. Some wire crates fold up, making them easy to move or store, and some are assembled with corner pins. Wire crates are relatively heavy. Folding plastic crates, such as those made by Nylabone, are also available. Plastic crates are, of course, lighter weight than the wire ones.

## Crate Size

How big should your dog's crate be? Big enough to let him stand, turn around, and lie down. If you're not sure what size to buy, ask your pup's breeder or other people who have dogs of similar size.

Construction quality is important. If you decide to purchase a wire crate, be sure that the wire is of a heavy enough gauge to withstand pushing or pulling by teeth, nose, and paws, and that the spacing between wires is close enough to prevent your puppy getting his head stuck. A bent wire or overly wide space can injure or even kill a pushy puppy. The same goes for the door. Make sure that the latch is secure and that clever little paws won't be able to slide it open—spring latches are safer than simple sliding ones. The door should fit snuggly into the opening so that your pup can't poke his head between the door and the frame.

## Crate Liners

You may want to pad the bottom of the crate, although some dogs seem to prefer the hard bottom and crumple up whatever padding is put inside. Be sure that your padding is washable—it can get pretty smelly if your dog goes out in the rain and mud and then lies in his crate. Among my favorite crate liners are rubber-backed bathroom rugs—they don't slip around, they're comfy, they come in great colors, and they wash well and last a long time.

## Crate Cautions

Your dog's crate should be a safe and pleasant place to be. It should never be used for punishment, and

*A crate, used properly, is a useful tool for housetraining, problem behavior prevention, and travel safety.*

*Your dog's crate should be a safe and pleasant place to be.*

no dog should ever be confined to a crate for more than a few hours a day. If you have to leave your dog for longer than about four hours, make arrangements for him to be out of the crate for at least a half hour of exercise, or find a safe way to confine him in a larger, more comfortable area.

## Leashes and Longlines

You won't get much training done if your dog wanders away two minutes into the lesson, so you need a leash for training. In fact, you need a leash for many occasions. For one thing, leashes keep dogs alive and in one piece. I wish I had a leash for every time I've heard about the dog who "never left my side" and then was killed the first time he did—I would hand them out to all the leashless dogs I see out and about. Leashes are also required by law in many places, and even if they weren't, a leash will keep your dog from disturbing wildlife, other people's pets, and people. I know it's hard to believe, but some people don't like dogs all that much, and even people who do like dogs don't like being chased when jogging or bicycling. So think of your dog's leash as not just a training tool but as a safety and etiquette tool as well.

Now the shopping dilemma—what kind of leash? One of those nylon jobs with the name of your favorite team emblazoned along its length? A neon-bright leash and matching collar ensemble? Plain but elegant leather? Let's discuss the various types out there and which are best for you and your dog.

If your dog will travel in your car a lot, you may find that it's more practical to buy two crates—one for the house and one for the car—than to have to move a single crate back and forth all the time, especially if your pup is large. Either plastic or wire will work in a car, although a plastic airline-approved crate will provide better protection for your dog in case of accident.

If you expect to fly your dog, you'll need an airline-approved crate. If your dog is small enough, you can carry him with you in the cabin in an approved carry-on carrier.

### Leather Leashes

For walks around the block, the choice of leash is yours, but for training, I recommend leather. It's easier on the hands and strong, and it will give you and your dog a good feel for one another's movements.

Many obedience instructors recommend a 6-foot (1.8-m) leash, and if you're going to buy only one leash, that's probably a good length. Personally I find 6-foot (1.8-m) leashes too long to manage easily except for teaching things that require a little distance from the dog. For most training (especially for teaching your dog to walk politely and for heeling), choose a leash that will keep your dog within 1 or 2 feet (0.3 or 0.6 m) of you without being tight when he's right beside you. The right length for you and your dog will depend on your relative heights, but for most people and dogs, a 2- to 4-foot (0.6- to 1.2-m) leash works well.

Leashes also come in a range of widths, and the proper width depends on the size of the dog. Most inexperienced owners use leashes that are heavier than they need, which makes the leash all that much harder to manage with one hand (which you need to do in training). If in doubt, ask your dog's breeder or an experienced obedience instructor for advice. Pay attention, too, to the size and weight of the slide bolt that fastens the leash to your dog's collar— don't weigh your dog down with a bolt that's huge in proportion to his own size!

### Longlines

There are times when a longline—essentially a super long leash—is useful. For instance, you can use a longline to teach your dog to come when called and to keep him safe while you practice *stays* in open areas. A longline can be whatever length you need it

*Your leash is an essential training tool that will keep your dog safe from many hazards of modern life.*

to be, from 10 feet (3.0 m) to 50 feet (15.2 m) or longer. You can purchase a longline from most pet supply stores or make one of inexpensive rope or clothesline. (Choose a size and texture that will be easy on your hands.)

### Retractable Leashes

An alternative to the longline is a retractable leash. Several types are available, all of which have a cord or nylon tape that retracts on a spring-loaded winding device housed in a plastic handle. One caution—check your retractable leash frequently for wear, especially to the thin cord and to connections. I have heard of serious injuries resulting from broken cords that snap back when retracted suddenly. Another problem with using a retractable leash in training is that it exerts constant tension on your dog's collar, which you may not want.

## Toys

Most dogs like toys. I like to have a couple of "special" toys that my dog gets to play with only when we're training—play is a reward.

### Types of Toys

Choose toys that will be easy for you to manage when you are also holding a leash and that suit your dog's size. Ideally, the toy you use in training should fit into a pocket so that you can pull it out quickly—as we shall see in Chapter 5, timing is everything, and rewards need to follow immediately after your dog does what you want him to do. Balls and other bouncy toys can be highly motivational, but they also can create chaos in the wrong setting, so use them judiciously. Stuffed toys, especially those with long appendages that are easy to grab, are popular with many dogs and trainers, as are braided tug toys. Nylabone makes some toys that serve as good play rewards as well.

### Toy Cautions

Be sure that whatever toys you use are too big for your dog to swallow or suck into his windpipe if he catches a direct toss. And speaking of tossed toys—don't toss anything hard directly at your dog unless you enjoy emergency vet runs for broken teeth.

## Treats

Most dogs are highly motivated by food. (If your dog truly isn't interested in food, find a toy or a certain ear scratch or something that makes him respond joyfully.) It's important to learn to use food as a reward, not a bribe—we'll talk more about that in Chapter 5.

### Types of Treats

The food you use in training should be very small and very attractive to your dog. It should also be easy to chew so that you don't have to stop and wait for your dog to stop chewing—training treats should go down the hatch without stopping the training. Variety is good—when your dog never knows for sure what his reward will be, he will stay more interested.

Some of the many treats that experienced trainers use include string cheese, very thinly sliced hotdogs, plain air-popped popcorn, tiny bits of cooked meat, tiny bits of veggies or fruits (my dog Rowdy would do anything for a piece of carrot), and of course tiny, soft dog treats. A small pouch on a belt works well for holding treats without getting your pockets all grubby.

### Treat Cautions

Two cautions about choosing treats. First, avoid additives that are not good for your dog, particularly sugar, salt, food dyes, and some artificial preservatives. Second, if your dog has a food allergy, check the ingredients of your treats as well as your dog food. (See Chapter 3.) Read the ingredients list, not just the hype.

## TRAINING CLASSES

Anyone who is serious about training a dog does most of the training at home—that's where we live with our dogs. But if you

Toys and play are motivational rewards for many dogs, but some dogs don't show a lot of interest in toys. Here is a way to make your dog take an interest in a training toy if he doesn't now. (The humans in your life may think you've gone off the deep end, but they'll recover.) Prerequisite: Your dog must be willing to give you things for this exercise. (See Chapter 8.)

- Find one special toy—like a tug rope or a stuffed toy—that your dog will get to play with only in training and only for short spurts.

- Put the toy in a drawer (or somewhere handy where your dog can't see it).

- Several times a day for the first day, when your dog is present, open the drawer and for a few seconds act excited about the toy inside.

- The next day, open the drawer and take the toy out for a few seconds, be very excited about holding it, and allow your dog to look but not touch.

- If your dog shows interest in your "treasure," spend a day or two getting it out and running around the room with it, hugging it, maybe tossing it in the air and catching it—the happier and more playful you are, the better. Let your dog have a very short sniff of the toy, but don't let him have it yet. (Do this at first with your dog on leash or confined to a smallish area.) By now, your dog should be pretty interested in your wonderful toy, so when you get it out of the drawer, play with it, then throw it and let your dog get it. After a few seconds, take the toy back and put it away.

How long the process takes will depend on your dog, but most dogs become very toy motivated in a few days. When your dog decides that he loves his training toy, you'll be able to use a few seconds of play with the toy as a reward in training. Two cautions, though. First, make sure the toy is too big for your dog to swallow because you will be tossing it to him in training. Second, bouncy toys like tennis balls may work if you're training alone out in the open, but use more "sedate" toys when training around other people and dogs or when indoors.

want your dog to respond to you not just at home but also at the park, the vet's office, and wherever else you take him, a class is your best option. The class environment simulates nonhome settings where your dog needs to ignore distractions, listen to you, and behave himself.

## Obedience Classes

A good dog-training class is a worthwhile investment in the future of your life with your dog. The time and money you spend on a class or two are a small fraction of what you will spend over your dog's lifetime, and they will no doubt save you time, money, and more than a little frustration over the years. A class environment provides for some of the socialization your dog needs (see Chapter 6) and teaches him to respond to you even with exciting distractions all around. A good instructor will help you become a more effective trainer and will point out mistakes that you don't even know you're making.

## *How to Find a Good Trainer*

The trick, of course, is to find a good class and good instructor. The dog-training industry is not regulated, and anyone can claim to be a trainer or obedience instructor, so it pays to check around before you sign up for a class. It's bad enough to waste money on a poor class, but your dog is also vulnerable to being frightened or even injured by the wrong person. If possible, observe a class or two before you sign up, and meet or observe your prospective instructor.

Here are some questions to ask when checking out a class or instructor. The answer to most of these questions should be yes.

- **Does the instructor have experience training dogs?** If possible, observe the instructor with her own dog or dogs. If she has an adult dog, is the dog well behaved? Does the dog usually obey? What does she do when the dog makes a mistake? If she has a puppy, is she patient but persistent when handling him? Yelling, hitting, shoving—rough methods in general—are a red light. And an instructor whose adult dog is poorly behaved probably can't help you train a good canine citizen.

- **Does the instructor have experience teaching obedience classes?** Long experience isn't necessarily a sign of knowledge

*Choose toys for your dog that are too big for him to swallow.*

*A good obedience instructor will help you become a more effective trainer.*

or good teaching skills, but your instructor should have some experience either teaching a class or assisting another instructor.

- **Does the instructor seem to be knowledgeable about dogs and dog training?** Has she attended seminars, workshops, and advanced classes? Does she read to keep up with the ever-growing body of knowledge about how dogs (and people) learn? Can she apply the knowledge she has or just spout theory and drop names?
- **Does the instructor communicate well?** Does she listen carefully and respond clearly? Does she offer help when someone has trouble getting a dog to respond? Can she get her own dog and the dogs in her class to do what she wants without resorting to extreme measures?
- **Does the instructor seem to really like dogs, people, and teaching?** Does she reward her students with praise and encourage them to do the same with their dogs? The last thing you and your dog need is someone who doesn't enjoy teaching you.
- **Is the instructor flexible?** A good dog trainer adapts to the individual dog and will help you figure out what works with your dog.

Take a look at the training facilities as well.

- **How big is the class?** If the class has more than ten people and dogs, will the instructor have a qualified assistant? Will you get individual help when you need it?

- **Are the facilities adequate?** Is there enough room to accommodate the class safely and comfortably? Is the place reasonably clean? Is the footing good so that you and your dog won't slip? Is the outdoor potty area reasonably clean?

- **Are policies in place to protect your dog's health?** All dogs should be required to show proof of proper veterinary care and to be reasonably clean and free of fleas.

- **Are policies and procedures in place to keep you and your dog safe?** If a dog in your class is aggressive toward other dogs or people, or if an owner cannot manage an overexuberant big dog, instructors should be ready and willing to take steps to keep other class members from being injured or frightened.

No matter how accomplished your instructor, always remember that your dog relies on you for his safety and well-being. If you are uncomfortable about doing something you're told to do, explain your concerns and ask for an alternative approach. In

*Obedience class enables your dog to socialize with other dogs and teaches him to respond to you despite distractions.*

addition, be cautious about who you allow to handle your dog. Many obedience instructors like to demonstrate techniques with dogs in their classes, and most of the time there's no problem. But if you have any reservation about allowing an instructor to take your dog from you, just say you'd rather not. And if you are uncomfortable about the instructor's knowledge, attitude, or methods, find a new class. Again, even if you walk away from part of the cost of the class, that's better than damaging your dog's trust in you and other people.

### Types of Training Classes

If you plan to continue training your dog beyond basic household obedience, you may want to look for a training facility or club that offers a consistent program of training from puppy basics through advanced levels. The details vary from place to place and instructor to instructor, but the following types of classes are commonly offered by private and club training programs.

- **Puppy kindergarten classes** are designed for puppies from about two to five months old. As we'll see in Chapter 6, young puppies can learn a lot. They also need to be socialized, and a good puppy class helps, especially if the puppies are given an opportunity to play together and to be handled by other people in the class. A caution here: All play among puppies should be closely supervised. Differences in size, age, and personality can be extreme during these months, and all puppies should come away from kindergarten with positive experiences, not fear or injury. Most puppy kindergarten classes teach basic skills (*leash walking, sit, down, come, beginning stay*) and offer discussions of housetraining, socialization, problem behaviors, and basic care.
- **Basic obedience classes** usually require the dogs to be five months old or older. A good basic obedience class is really a people-training class—it will teach you how to train your dog. In addition, classes provide an opportunity for continued

*Basic obedience classes focus on basic skills, such as walking nicely on leash.*

socialization and give you the support of a good instructor and fellow dog owners. Most basic classes focus on—you guessed it!—basic commands and skills, including walking politely on a leash, paying attention to the handler, sitting, lying down, and staying on the first command, coming when called, and depending on the dog's progress, perhaps some work off leash. While a puppy kindergarten class may introduce some of these skills, very young dogs lack the attention span and physical control and coordination necessary to master them. Some basic classes aim at specific goals, like preparing your dog to pass the American Kennel Club (AKC) Canine Good Citizen (CGC) test (see Chapter 10) or to proceed to more advanced training in obedience, agility, or other sports.

- **Competition obedience classes** teach you to train your dog to compete in obedience trials. They focus on handling skills as well

*Practicing at home is vital for success in obedience classes.*

as techniques for teaching the dog advanced exercises (jumping, retrieving, and so forth). Competition obedience classes are usually split up according to the level of training.

- **Agility classes** teach you how to train and handle your dog over jumps, tunnels, dog walks, A-frames, and other obstacles used in agility. As we discussed in Chapter 3, your dog's bones should be finished growing before he tries some of the obstacles.
- **Handling classes** prepare you and your dog to show in conformation shows. Running a dog around the ring and having him stand and look gorgeous isn't as easy as it looks!
- **Other specialized classes and seminars** are available for training your dog to hunt, work livestock, track, go-to-ground, course or race, pull, and perform other activities. If you're interested in a specialized sport, ask your breeder, veterinarian, or other people with dogs of your breed or similar breeds about classes or private instruction in your area.

If you do plan to go on to compete in obedience, agility, conformation, or other sports, be sure to tell your instructor what your goals are. If possible, find an instructor who participates in your sport or sports of choice. She can help you lay the groundwork for advanced training during early obedience training and help you avoid forming habits you will have to break later.

Beware of any school or trainer who claims to be able to train your dog completely in just a few weeks. One time through basic obedience isn't enough for most dogs—or people! Training takes time, and if the claims seem too good to be true, they are. If you decide to take another basic class or to go on to specialized training, consider taking classes from more than one instructor so that you get more than one point of view. Eventually you will develop your own style of training—or styles if you train more than one dog.

## Training at Home

You will do most of your training at home, of course. Once a week in class just won't do it—you and your dog both need to practice what you learn in class.

Practice doesn't need to occur all at once or eat up big blocks of time. In fact, several short sessions of ten minutes or so scattered throughout the day are more effective and less tiresome for both you and your dog. If you're watching television in the evening, use the commercials to work on one command. Five minutes here and there quickly add up to better-trained dog.

As we shall see, you can also take advantage of training opportunities whenever you interact with your dog. Whether you train in class or on your own, though, training will make your dog a better-behaved, happier, and more confident companion. As a bit of conventional wisdom among dog trainers goes, the most loving thing you can do for your dog is to train him.

The right training tools can make an enormous difference in your training efforts and life in general with your dog. You don't need to spend a fortune or have the top of the line, but do invest in the things that will keep your dog safe, enhance your life with him, and promote good behavior and training. You, your dog, and the people in your lives will all be happier as a result.

# 5

# TRAINING TECHNIQUES

There are many, many ways to train a dog, and trying to decide on the best way to train can be confusing. The fact is, no "best method" exists. Some methods work for some dogs and not for others. Some people train well with one method but not another. Many experienced trainers use a grab-bag of techniques, adapting their approach to the individual dog and situation.

In this and future chapters, I will explain some methods that have worked for me. The emphasis in this book is on positive methods that motivate your dog by rewarding him when he's correct. I do not recommend punishment (leash jerking, yelling, hitting, or other strong-arm approaches), but once the dog has learned a command, I do use quick "corrections," such as gently leading him back to where he's supposed to be or a firm "ah ah" that means "oops, you got that wrong." (I'll explain more about corrections later in the chapter.)

Training should get you the results you want in a reasonable amount of time, but it is an ongoing process, and a well-trained dog does not happen overnight. Training should also be fun for both of you. Okay, there will be times when you or your dog or both of you are frustrated and not having all that much fun. But overall, you should look forward to the time you spend training your furry friend, and he should do the happy dance when he sees the training leash in your hand.

Dog-training techniques have undergone a revolution over the past few decades. Modern dog trainers use a variety of methods to get the results they want, but the best and most effective trainers understand the six principles of successful training, motivate their dogs, show their dogs what they want, forgive mistakes, and take advantage of learning opportunities whenever they occur. Let's examine these techniques in more detail.

## UNDERSTAND THE SIX PRINCIPLES OF SUCCESSFUL TRAINING

Whatever tools and methods you use with a particular dog, training will go easier for both of you if you apply six basic principles: consistency, conciseness, generosity, intelligence, preparation, and the joy of being with your dog through thick and thin.

Positive, motivational dog training is based on the premise that behavior that is rewarded becomes habitual, and behavior that is not rewarded diminishes or disappears.

*Training with motivation and rewards is much more effective—and fun!—than using punishment and intimidation.*

## 1. Be Consistent

When training, apply the same rules and use the same words all the time. Switching signals on your dog just isn't fair and will confuse him. And human language is not his natural means of communication, so give him a break. If you want him to come, say "Come" every time, not "Come," "Come here," or "Get over here" (and don't use "Come" to mean "Let's go for a walk").

## 2. Be Concise

Give your command just once. Repeating a command over and over teaches your dog to ignore it because you obviously don't really care if he does it or not. At least not until the tenth time, when you scream and put your fists on your hips.

## 3. Be Generous

Reward your dog for being right. As we'll see later in this book, you won't always give a treat every time your dog does what you tell him, but you still need to reward him at least part of the time. Remember, not all rewards are edible—verbal praise, an ear massage, and a good butt scratch all count.

## 4. Be Smart

Don't give a command unless you either are confident that your dog understands it and will respond to it correctly, or you are in a position to help him get it right. For example, if your dog is just learning to come when called, and you know that he responds in training only half the time, don't use your *come* command when he's in the yard and you're in the doorway wrapped in a bath towel. Remember, he's learning all the time, and if you can't correct his mistakes, he learns that he doesn't really have to obey. So don't keep calling him while he ignores you. Get dressed and go get him.

## 5. Be Prepared

If you are prepared for the possibility that your dog won't come when you call (because he hasn't yet learned to come every time in training), you won't have to get dressed and go after your dog. You will have a longline by the back door, and you will fasten it to your dog's collar before you send him out to potty so that you can call once, then reel him in and reward him when he gets to you.

## 6. Be Happy

Dog training is not an adversarial event. Your dog is your friend and your training partner, so be happy when you tell him what to do. Don't growl—keep your voice upbeat and smile at him. Dogs are very sensitive to our tone of voice and body language, so use both to let your partner know that you will be oh so happy when he does what you tell him.

## MOTIVATE YOUR DOG

Hopefully you are motivated to train your dog by the knowledge that training will make for a better-behaved companion and a closer bond between the two of you. But what about your dog? Why should he care about learning to come when you call him? Look at it from his perspective—you'll still be there in ten minutes when he's finished sniffing that fascinating patch of weeds at the back of the yard. What's your hurry?

For some reason, a lot of people think that dogs should automatically want to obey. But your dog is not a robot. He's a thinking, feeling being with complex drives and desires. Coming when you call, or lying down, or doing whatever you're telling him to do has no inherent value to him. It's up to you to motivate him

**When Your Dog Doesn't Seem to Be Listening**

There are times when a dog won't come or lie down or do anything you tell him, and that can be frustrating. When that happens, ask yourself why. Does he need a good run to take the edge off? Is he really excited about something? Is he focused on doing something that his genes tell him he just has to do? Whatever you do, don't give up. Review Chapters 2 and 3, be patient with your furry friend, and keep training. It's all part of life with dogs.

by showing him why doing what you say is good for him. The best way to do that is through *positive reinforcement*, which is the process of rewarding your dog with something he likes for doing what you want him to do. Some trainers use "pure" positive reinforcement, meaning that they never use corrections in training. Most use a combination of positive reinforcement for correct behaviors and fair, gentle corrections for unwanted behaviors (which include not doing what you told him to do).

## Rewards

A *reward*—or in psychological terms, a *reinforcer*—is simply something that your dog gets as a result of behaving in a certain way. Rewards are used extensively in positive training to motivate learning and occasionally, later, to reinforce established behaviors.

Some behaviors offer inherent rewards—eating satisfies hunger (or greed), urinating relieves pressure on the bladder, and running and playing feel good. Other behaviors, including a lot of those we humans like our dogs to perform, offer no natural rewards. Fortunately, you can provide the rewards to reinforce the behaviors you want from your dog.

### *Types of Rewards*

*Toys and play are very motivating for most dogs.*

What is a reward to your dog? Food is probably the most

## Treats to Try

When choosing treats for training, keep in mind that they count as part of your dog's diet—they add calories, and if your dog has dietary restrictions due to allergies or health issues, the treats shouldn't violate those restrictions. Whatever you use, keep the pieces very small. The point is not to feed your dog but to reward him. Treats should be soft and easy to chew so that your dog doesn't have to stop training to chew. Make a "trail mix" of different treats so that your dog never knows what the next flavor will be. Here are some treats to try:

- single bits of your dog's regular kibble
- plain toasted oats-type cereal (no sugar, please)
- cheese—string cheese, cheese cubes ("squeeze cheese" in a can is good for some purposes)
- tiny vegetable bits—carrots and green beans work well
- tiny bits of cooked meat—liver, chicken, beef
- commercial treats made for training

obvious and most commonly used reward, although some dogs have very little interest in working for treats, especially when they are stressed. A chance to play with a ball or other toy, such as a Nylabone, is rewarding for many dogs. Butt scratches delight some dogs, and a high-pitched human voice makes some dogs wriggle and wag. A few dogs are satisfied with a quiet word of praise from their handlers. In short, a reward (or reinforcer) is whatever provides your individual dog enough satisfaction to motivate him to learn or perform for you.

Here's an experiment for you to try even before you begin serious training. Find out what tickles your dog—what makes his eyes sparkle and his tail wag? My dog Rowdy loved to be patted and scratched just above the base of his tail and would work happily for bits of carrot. Jay will do anything for a tiny bit of cheese. Magic likes me to talk in a "silly" high-pitched, fast voice. Find several different things that you will be able to use to reward your dog—a special food, a toy, an action, a voice. Put them in your "reward repertoire," and keep adding to it as you discover new pleasures for your dog.

### Primary Versus Secondary Reinforcers

We won't spend a lot of time on technical language, but it is important to understand the difference between what psychologists call *primary reinforcers* and *secondary reinforcers*. A primary reinforcer is one that the learner values by nature—food, for example. A secondary reinforcer is one that has acquired value for the learner by being associated with a primary reinforcer. If you tell your dog to sit and tell him "Good job," the words mean nothing to him (although he may like your tone of voice and body language if they convey happiness). But if you simultaneously give your dog a treat (the primary reinforcer or reward) and tell him "Good job," he will learn to value the words "good job," and they will be rewarding to him even without the treat.

### How to Use Rewards in Training

Rewards are used in training to show the dog in tangible form that he's done something right. As your dog learns and becomes reliable on a particular command, it's important to stop giving a reward every time and begin giving rewards on an irregular, random schedule. In other words, when you first start to teach a command—*sit*, for example—you should give a treat every time your dog sits on command. But as he masters that lesson, you should treat him less and less often. Studies have shown that random rewards reinforce behavior better than constant rewards. The example often used is the contrast between a slot machine and a vending machine. People will feed coins into a slot machine time after time, even though they are rewarded with a win only occasionally. But if a vending machine offers no "reward," most people stop dropping coins in on the first or second failure. Your dog is the same way. If he's used to getting a treat every time he sits, and you are in a situation

*Consistency and timing are essential for effective training.*

*A reward, whether treats or play, is used in training to show a dog he's done something right.*

where you have no treats, he will stop obeying very quickly if he gets nothing in return. But if he knows there's a chance of a reward, he'll gamble that maybe this is the time.

## Markers

A *marker* is a signal, usually auditory but sometimes visual or tactile, that indicates, or marks, a very specific action or behavior. For our purposes, I will use the term *marker* to indicate something specific that signals to your dog that he's done the right thing and a reward is on the way. The term *mark* refers to your act of signaling. The marker works as a bridge between the behavior you want and the reward you provide, so mark immediately *after* your dog does what you want, not before.

### Types of Markers

Your marker can be:

• a clicker if you want to try one (they are readily available at pet

supply stores)

- a specific word or phrase (pick one you don't use all the time so that it stands out in your dog's mind—"Good job!" or "Pretty" or "Excellent" work well)
- a whistle (this is a good option for distance work but would be really annoying to other people in a class or group-practice situation)
- a visual signal (I don't recommend this for general use, but if you are training a deaf dog, a small flashlight can be used as a marker)

### Loading the Marker

Before you can use a marker to tell your dog he's right, you need to teach him what the marker means. This process is called loading. Begin by simply marking a very simple behavior—perhaps a slight turn of the head to the left—and offering a reward. (Food works best as a reward at this early stage.) Don't ask your dog to do anything in particular; just repeat several loading sets over the course of a day or two: mark | treat, mark | treat, mark | treat. Then, before each training session, "reload" your marker by repeating the mark treat sequence a few times. At first you will give a treat every time you use your marker, but eventually you will be able to treat only sporadically because the marker itself will tell your dog that he's doing what you want, and a reward is coming eventually.

### Using the Marker

Suppose you want to teach your dog to sit on command by

### Clicker Training

In recent years, many dog trainers have employed a training approach called *clicker training* because a handheld clicker (a device that makes a sharp click) is used as a secondary, or learned, reinforcer. Clicker training is based on a form of learning that psychologists call *operant conditioning*, in which the dog learns to associate a marker (in this case, the sound of the click) with a reward. In practice, this means that when your dog does what you want, you mark his behavior with the marker, and then you reward him.

Many good arguments can be made for using a clicker as a marker. The sound is distinct from the sounds of everyday life, and evidence suggests that the sharp click may affect the dog's brain differently and more profoundly than the sound of a human voice. The clicker also helps to make you, the trainer, conscious of your timing, which is essential for effective use of a marker in training. On the other hand, if you don't have a lot of experience training dogs, you probably already feel like you need a third hand to manage your leash, your dog, and your treats. Adding a handheld clicker to the equation can be overwhelming. Also, most people don't have a clicker at the ready for every training opportunity that arises. Remember there are other ways to mark desired behavior.

marking the *sit* with a clicker. There are different ways to do this, but for simplicity, let's say that you simply watch your dog closely, and when he sits on his own, you immediately click and give him a reward. Then you wait until he sits on his own again, click immediately, and reward him. It won't be long until he figures out that he has trained you to click and give him a treat by placing his fanny on the floor! When he is repeatedly sitting (and drooling, no doubt!), begin to say "Sit" when you see him start to lower his rear end. Then mark by clicking as soon as he sits, and reward him. When that works consistently, you can start to give the command "Sit" and to mark and reward the behavior when he does it right. You also can start to ignore him when he sits without being told. In other words, now he is learning that you really only care about him sitting when you say that word.

Finally, you need a way to tell your dog when he's finished with something. Suppose you tell him to lie down and stay. How will he know when he's allowed to get up? If you let him decide that five minutes is long enough on this rug, then why not five seconds? You'll be happier and your dog will be more secure about what you expect if you make the decisions. When you tell your dog to lie down or sit, he should remain in that position until you tell him he's free to do something else. In pure operant conditioning, the marker signals both correct behavior and the end of the required behavior. In other words, if you say "Down" and "Stay," then wait one minute and mark the behavior, you are telling your dog simultaneously that he did it right, and now he's free to move. But if, like most dog trainers, you use a combination of techniques, you will need a release word that tells your dog he's off the hook for now. Many people use the word "okay," which is fine except that it's very easy to accidentally release your dog by saying "okay" to someone other than your dog. I recommend that you use a word or very short phrase that you don't use often in general conversation. The word itself isn't important—I use "free" and have heard "go play," "at ease," and my favorite, "thank you!"

### Timing

Timing is critical when training because you need to mark the exact behavior you want. Suppose you are teaching your dog to sit on command, and you are luring him into a *sit* with a piece of food. He puts his fanny on the floor and immediately stands back up.

If you mark the behavior at that point, you're too late—you have marked his standing up, not his sitting. So pay close attention to exactly what you mark and reward to be sure that you are teaching your dog what you want him to learn.

# SHOW YOUR DOG WHAT YOU WANT

No matter how brilliant your dog may be, you can't hand him written instructions for a self-study course in obedience. Talking louder won't work either—you can scream "SIT" until you pass out, but if your dog doesn't understand what you want him to do, he'll comply only by accident. You're going to have to show him what you want him to do. Five approaches are commonly used to teach specific behaviors, and many trainers alternate these approaches or use them in various combinations. In other words, use whatever works best.

*Modeling in training involves physically guiding your dog into the action or position you want him to perform.*

## 1. Modeling

No, I'm not going to tell you how your dog can become a glamorous collar model, although if he learns enough interesting behaviors, that might be a possibility. *Modeling* in training means physically positioning or moving the dog as you want him to do eventually on his own.

### How Modeling Works

Modeling in training involves positioning your dog. If you gently push his fanny down as you say "Sit," you are modeling the *sit* command.

### Advantages

Modeling is useful for teaching a few behaviors (like

*shake hands*, for instance), but some are too awkward for modeling, and you cannot model a behavior that your dog does at any distance from you.

### Disadvantages

Modeling is used a lot to teach things to people, and it works in part because we can say "Put your arm here" to convey the complete idea. But you can't do that with your dog. As a result, he may learn to sit on command, or he may learn that "sit" means "now she's going to push my butt down." He may not learn to associate "sit" with any behavior on his part and may simply rely on you to position him. Finally, he may resist being physically positioned. In addition, forcing a dog into some positions or movements could cause pain, discomfort, or even injury. Modeling should be employed only rarely—your dog will learn more if he performs the behavior you want on his own.

## 2. Luring

One way to get your dog to perform a specific behavior on his own is by *luring*, or enticing, him with a reward, usually a treat or toy.

### How Luring Works

If you want to teach your dog to spin to the right, for instance, you might lure him in a circle to the right with a treat.

### Advantages

Luring is an inherently positive and motivational way to teach, and by holding the lure in your moving hand, you teach a hand signal that can eventually be used without the treat.

*Luring involves enticing your dog to perform an action with the promise of a visible reward, usually a treat or toy. This dog's trainer is luring her dog into a down.*

### Disadvantages

One problem with luring is that your dog may become so focused on the food that he doesn't really learn the command—he appears to because he "assumes the position," but he's just following his nose without using his brain. He may also become dependent on your hand movements and not learn the verbal command. Hand signals are great, but they only work if your dog is looking at you. Another disadvantage is that luring is useful only when your dog is close to you. It's very easy to become dependent on the lure, turning it into a bribe (and turning your dog into an extortionist who won't perform unless he has a cookie in his face). I like to use a lure to start teaching certain behaviors, but I quickly remove it when the dog begins to offer the behavior on his own.

## 3. Shaping

*Shaping* is a process in which you break down a desired behavior into tiny increments. At first you reward your dog for performing a teensy bit of the behavior; then, when he performs that action repeatedly, you up the ante, waiting for him to do a bit more.

Shaping can be used to teach your dog complex behaviors and to perform when he's at some distance from you (as long as he can hear the marker).

### How Shaping Works

Let's look at teaching the spin to the right again. You patiently wait for your dog to turn his head, even slightly, to the right. Then you mark that behavior and reward him. When he makes the connection between turning his head and the marker and reward, he will repeatedly turn his head. When he is doing that consistently, you wait until he turns it a bit farther before you mark and reward. Eventually, you wait until he turns his head all the way around, which will cause him to spin his body, too (unless he's in a horror movie). There's no correction for not performing—in fact, your only reaction is to wait. When he is spinning consistently, you add a cue (command or name) a split second before he spins. Do that a number of times, and soon you'll be able to say "Rowdy, spin," and around he will go.

*Don't forget to take time for play during training sessions—training should be fun for both you and your dog, even if it's sometimes frustrating.*

*Play is an effective training reward.*

### Advantages

Shaping requires you to be patient, but because this technique encourages your dog to think for himself and figure things out, once he learns to associate what he does with what you say and do, he will be less confused and more reliable in responding to commands. Also, once your dog catches on to the game, it will be a lot easier to get him to repeat behaviors that make you mark and treat. He will also think his way through learning new things. Although shaping purists do not lure new behaviors, you can combine the mark-and-treat benefits of shaping with luring to speed things up.

### Disadvantages

Shaping can be frustrating, especially when both you and your dog are new at it. Your timing has to be precise so that you mark while your dog is turning his head to the right, not when he's swinging it back to the left. And your dog has to make the connection between his behavior and your response. (In a sense, he learns that he can make you do something for him—mark and treat.)

## 4. Targeting

*Targeting* teaches a dog to touch a specific object to earn a reward (a treat at first, then verbal rewards punctuated by occasional treats). The target can be whatever you want it to be—a stick, a plastic lid, a piece of tape on the wall, your hand. In fact, once your dog understands the concept, you can easily switch targets for different purposes.

### How Targeting Works

Targeting is the process of teaching a dog to go to or touch an object. It's used frequently to teach the dog to perform complicated movements—for instance, to spin in a circle or move away from the handler. (For a step-by-step guide to teaching your dog to target, see Chapter 7.)

### Advantages

Targeting is extremely useful for teaching behaviors that involve motion or that require the dog to move away from you. Not only can you teach him lots of cute tricks, but if you decide to train for competition obedience, agility, or some other sports, you can use targets to teach advanced behaviors.

### Disadvantages

You do have to wean the target away once your dog understands what you want him to do so that he doesn't rely on the target to perform.

## 5. Capturing

*Capturing* is the process of reinforcing a behavior that your dog performs spontaneously by marking the behavior and rewarding it. It works best with a dog who has experience with learning through shaping so that he understands that something he did caused you to mark and treat. He will then try various behaviors as he figures out which one you're after.

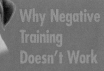

### How Capturing Works

As with shaping, do not give a cue for the behavior until your dog figures out which behavior you want and does it consistently. Then, just as he's about to do it, add your cue (like "Scratch your ear!"), then mark when he does it and give him a treat.

### Advantages

Capturing is an excellent way to teach your dog to perform behaviors that you can't teach by other methods. For example, suppose you want your dog to sneeze or shake or scratch his ear on cue—capturing is the way to go.

### Disadvantages

The only real disadvantage to capturing as a training method is that it requires patience because it may take a long time for your dog to do what you're waiting for him to do.

## FORGIVE MISTAKES

Training doesn't always go smoothly, of course. Your dog will make mistakes as he learns, and you will make mistakes as you train him. In fact, if you are a novice or rusty trainer, chances are your mistakes will cause a lot of your dog's mistakes. Stop and think about what you are doing and how it affects your dog, and keep in mind how hard it is to learn something new—like how to train your dog. It isn't easy to manage a leash, rewards, your own feet, the command, your timing—whew! Now imagine that your instructor is a member of another species who communicates with beeps and clucks and who wants you to do some very silly things, and you have some idea of the task your dog faces. When you get frustrated, quit for a while. Then begin again, and enjoy the process.

### Mistakes Are Good

Now, let me qualify that. Mistakes are good if they are pointed out and contrasted against the times your dog performs an exercise correctly. Suppose he is learning to sit and to lie down on command. You've been practicing both commands, and it's time for another short practice session. You have a treat in your hand and you say "Sit." Your dog makes a mistake—he lies down and smiles at you expectantly, waiting for his reward. You turn and walk away a few steps, and he follows. You stop and say "Sit." This time he thinks for a second, then sits his butt on the floor, the same silly grin on his face. Voilà! You mark his *sit* and give him the treat. You play with him for a moment, then say "Sit," and he responds correctly. You mark his *sit*, and this time you give him several treats as a jackpot, scratch his ears, and settle back on the couch for the next segment of your favorite television show.

What just happened? Your dog made a mistake, testing his understanding of the word "sit," and he learned that it means "fanny on floor but not elbows." Without such mistakes, your dog will have a difficult time differentiating the correct from the incorrect behavior. With mistakes, he can refine his understanding, and a dog who really understands the commands will respond to them reliably rather than by dumb luck.

*Mistakes while learning are normal, but when your dog knows a command, he must learn to obey it.*

## Do-Overs—What to Do When Your Dog Is Wrong

Mistakes while learning are perfectly understandable, but there comes a time when your dog knows a command and must learn that he has no choice but to obey it. Quick responses by your dog are usually a matter of convenience for you, but there are times when obedience is a matter of your dog's life and death—like when he is standing in harm's way and you need him to come to you immediately. He has to understand that he can't choose to obey you sometimes if he feels like it and blow you off otherwise.

Am I suggesting that you rough up your dog? Absolutely not! Rough and abusive training tactics—yelling, jerking with a leash, hitting, kicking, rolling, and so forth—have no place in dog training. (In fact, those methods are counterproductive.) If you want to hit or kick, sign up for a boxing or martial arts class. I *am* suggesting that you correct your dog for making mistakes if you are sure that he understands the command you have asked him to perform.

With the rise of positive training methods, "correction" has become a dirty word among some dog trainers, no doubt because of heavy-handed training tactics that used to be common. But the truth is that dogs need to be told not only when they get something right but also when they don't. And once they know the difference, they need to be held responsible for their own behavior. Some of the most confused, unhappy-looking dogs around are those who don't know that they are absolutely, positively required to do what they're told. We need to provide loving leadership; dogs without leaders are rarely happy dogs.

*A fair correction might include gently leading your dog back to your side if he strays on leash while walking together.*

I will explain corrections for specific problems later in this book,

but for now, four things always apply when it comes to corrections (and I rarely say always or never!):

1. Corrections should never inflict pain or fear.
2. Corrections should be fair—don't correct your dog for not doing something he doesn't understand.
3. Corrections should be immediate—if you see your dog make the mistake, correct him; otherwise, forgive, forget, and take steps to keep him from repeating it.
4. Corrections should be unemotional—anger, like bullying, has no place in your relationship with your dog.

Fair and appropriate corrections may include, for instance, saying "ah ah," gently leading your dog back to where he was supposed to stay, or guiding him gently over a jump or through a tunnel that he ran around. A correction should be thought of as a reminder and explanation of a boo-boo, not as a punishment. After all, have you ever learned to do anything without making a single mistake?

*Take advantage of training opportunities as they come up both during and outside of formal training sessions. This dog's trainer can use this opportunity to reinforce the* off *command.*

## TAKE ADVANTAGE OF LEARNING OPPORTUNITIES

We humans tend to compartmentalize our activities and to think of each one happening at a specific time—time to eat a meal, time to go to work, time to train the dog. And there is certainly nothing wrong with scheduling a specific time for dog training—I encourage you to make several 20- to 30-minute "appointments" with your dog each week, especially when you are teaching him new things. But remember that, whether you are "officially" training or not, your dog is learning.

*Your dog should obey your command no matter what he's doing.*

In the short training session described earlier, you persisted with training the *sit* until your dog got it right. Now suppose that instead of hanging out in front of the television, you and your dog followed the training session with a nice evening walk. You stop to talk to Mrs. Johnson down the street, and you tell your dog to sit. He sniffs Mrs. Johnson, bounces to the end of his leash, pees on a rock, and rushes the other way to sniff a tree. He does just about everything except what you told him to do. What did he just learn?

If you want your dog to obey you only when he's "in class" or when he feels like it, that's up to you. Personally, if I give my dog a command that he knows, I expect him to do it no matter where we are. So, I would ask Mrs. Johnson to hold that thought for a moment. Then I would shorten my leash, remind my dog to sit, and mark his correct behavior.

Training opportunities are all around you, so take advantage of them as they come up. If you're teaching your dog to sit on command, have him sit for his dinner, to get his leash on for a walk, at the door before he goes out, and at intersections when you're out for a walk. Have him practice *stays* while you dust the furniture or eat your dinner or shine your shoes. Have him lie down or stand before you throw his ball. Practicing commands in different situations will help him understand that "sit" means "put your fanny on the floor," whether he's outdoors or in the basement or a block from home on a walk or at training class. Switching commands in each situation will ensure that he sits or lies down because that's the command you gave, not because you have his food bowl in your hand.

While he is learning, you'll have to take the time to mark and reward correct responses and to remind your dog when he's wrong, but that investment of your time for a few months will pay huge dividends. He will be happier because he knows what's expected of him, and you'll be happier because your dog is well behaved and responsive.

# 6

## PUPPY TRAINING

Your puppy may be the most perfect creature you've ever laid eyes on, but he won't be perfectly trained unless you take the time to teach him what he needs to know. He comes with instincts that tell him to do certain things, a heart that makes him want to be your best friend, and the intelligence to learn what he needs to know. He does not come with a fluent understanding of human language, etiquette, or sensibilities. Even human babies have to learn those things—how could you expect more of your canine baby?

Fortunately, puppies are eager to learn. Exactly how your puppy approaches the learning process will depend on his genetic heritage (terriers approach life differently from the way retrievers do, for example) and on his individual personality, but certain principles apply to training all puppies. As we have seen, everything in your puppy's life affects his ability to learn what you want him to learn—his environment, nutrition, health, and contact with dogs, people, and other animals all influence his mental, physical, and social development. If you plan ahead and set the stage to encourage good behavior all the time (well, nearly all the time) and to prevent or discourage unwanted behavior, you'll make things a lot easier on your puppy and on yourself, and you will help him develop into the best dog he can be.

At first glance, it may not seem that socialization has anything to do with housetraining or that puppy kindergarten class will help with crate training. The fact is, though, that these essential components of a good canine education all work together to help your puppy develop into a confident, well-behaved adult dog. And if you have an adult dog whose early education was a bit lacking, don't despair! With patience and persistence, you can use this chapter to work on his inner puppy and help him develop to his best potential.

## UNDERSTANDING PUPPY DEVELOPMENT

Puppies are not just small, cute versions of adult dogs. They are canine "children," and like their human counterparts, they go through distinct developmental stages on their way to adulthood. If you are raising a puppy, understanding these stages will better equip you

*Your puppy's education began long before you brought him home. This little mixed breed has already learned a lot from the dogs and people he has known in his short life.*

to help him develop his full potential. If you are training an older puppy or an adult, you may gain some insights into his behavior by understanding how he developed. So let's begin with a basic overview of puppy development.

## Weeks of Development

Say the word "puppy" and most people see a mental image of a growing canine about six to eight weeks old. It's easy to think that your puppy's life began the day you took him home, but those preceding weeks since his birth, and even the nine weeks he spent in utero, have a lifelong influence on his health and behavior. It may help you as a dog owner and trainer to understand how puppies develop during their earliest weeks on earth.

### Weeks 1 and 2

For the first two weeks after they are whelped (born), puppies cannot see or hear, but their noses work very well, enabling them to root out their mother's milk and to recognize familiar dogs and humans who hold and nuzzle them. A newborn puppy cannot

shiver to warm himself or pant to cool himself, so he relies on his environment to maintain his body temperature. He can and will snuggle with his siblings and crawl toward or away from warmth provided by a heat lamp or heating pad. He cannot urinate or defecate without direct stimulation, which his dam (mother) normally provides. In fact, the neonatal puppy depends completely on his dam or foster dam for safety, nourishment, bodily functions, warmth, and cleanliness.

The canine mother depends in turn on the breeder for good nutrition and health care, a safe, private, and clean environment, and plenty of emotional support and cuddles. A good breeder also handles the puppies frequently and provides neurological stimulation that helps them develop more brain cells and prepare for later learning.

### Week 3

The third week of a puppy's life brings many changes. His eyes and ears open, and he begins to respond to light, movement, and sounds. He is easily startled by the sudden onslaught of stimuli and should not be exposed to sudden movements, loud noises, or bright or flashing lights (including camera flashes). The three-week-old puppy crawls around the "den" and is very aware of his littermates and his dam, people, other animals who visit the puppies, and toys or other objects in the whelping area. By the end of the third week, he may even try to play with his siblings and with toys. If he's a bold puppy, he may try to escape from the whelping box to explore the bigger world. He begins to stand and walk, although like any toddler he sways, staggers, and falls down a lot. He grows quickly

### Your Puppy's Attention Span

Whether you are teaching new things or practicing earlier lessons, remember that puppies have short attention spans. Let your puppy's own abilities guide you. If he loses interest after ten minutes, then ten minutes is enough for him at one time. If he's still focused at 20 minutes, then it's fine to train for 20 minutes. Either way, don't make him do one thing over and over again for 10 or 20 minutes—you'll both be bored silly. Instead, when he does something correctly once or twice, reward him, play with him, and move on to something else or quit for a while.

*Your puppy's dam (mother) had a profound effect on your puppy's early social education. This Pomeranian mother clearly loves her puppies.*

and gains considerable strength and coordination during the third week, and he can begin to learn to accept gentle grooming with a soft brush, as well as nail trimming.

### Week 4 (Through Week 7)

Beginning at four weeks of age and ending at seven weeks, a puppy experiences many changes, and he may leave for a new life at the end of this period. He learns to eat solid food and to drink water rather than relying on his dam. The urge for cleanliness that is present in most puppies kicks in, and he begins to go to a remote spot to urinate and defecate. If he's lucky, his breeder helps the puppy begin housetraining by keeping the puppy area clean, and weather permitting, by taking him outdoors to eliminate beginning in the fourth or fifth week.

He also begins to learn the social skills he will need throughout his life. He learns to communicate with and understand his dam, siblings, and perhaps other dogs, and the people in his life. He forms bonds. He asserts his personality and assumes his own position in the social hierarchy of the litter. He spends a lot of time playing and play fighting with his siblings, and he learns from them and from his mother that life includes discipline and that behavior has consequences. His mother and siblings reprimand him when he bites too hard, teaching him the essential trait of bite inhibition (self-control of the urge to bite). His problem-solving skills develop, especially if the breeder provides a variety of toys and small obstacles such as cardboard boxes, barriers, steps, and other challenges. He becomes more coordinated, and faster.

During the fourth week, the puppy's sensory development accelerates. He now recognizes and responds to people, and he begins to learn how to bond to people and other dogs. He is alert and easily startled and should be sheltered from influences that could frighten him and have long-lasting effects. He learns very quickly from the fourth through eighth weeks, and he remembers what he learns—critical skills for survival as a wild canid. An environment rich in playthings—a variety of toys, rolled-up towels to crawl over, shredded newspaper to dig into, tunnels to crawl through, and so on—help him develop his ability to learn. He should be exposed to the sounds of life—radio, television, music, toys that make noise, washers and dryers, vacuum cleaners, and so forth—beginning during the fourth week.

### Week 5 (Through Week 7)

Beginning during the fifth week and ending no earlier than seven weeks, the puppy needs to spend most of his time with his siblings, and some with his dam, to learn essential canine social skills. He also needs some individual human attention to help him learn to bond to people.

### Week 6 (Through Week 7)

Exposure to more new experiences will benefit the puppy during his sixth and seventh weeks—the hair dryer, short car rides, carefully screened human visitors, and exposure to the breeder's gentle adult dogs other than the puppy's dam. At this age, the puppy can begin short, positive training sessions, learning some basic skills (*stand*, *sit*, *come*) and—more importantly—learning to learn.

### Weeks 7 and 8

Puppies learn faster between seven and eight weeks of age than at any other time in their lives, and they retain an amazing amount of the information they acquire during these weeks. If you consider the life of a wild canid, this makes perfect sense. Pups leave the

As tempting as it is to bring that adorable fluff ball home as early as possible, remember that a puppy will be a "toddler" for only about a month out of a lifetime of a decade or more. Don't sacrifice his critical developmental period for a couple of weeks of cuteness. If you can't devote the time he needs to early training and socialization, it may be better to wait another couple of weeks before you bring him home. (Be sure, of course, that the breeder is committed to handling the puppies properly during this period.)

den and begin to explore the world at around seven weeks, but that world is a dangerous and unforgiving place. The pup who doesn't learn quickly dies. Fortunately, most domestic puppies live in safer environments than their wild cousins, and they get to repeat the lessons they fail the first time around.

## So When Can You Bring Your Puppy Home?

A widespread idea persists that you must take your puppy home at exactly seven weeks of age or he will never bond to you and your family. Not true! That idea comes from a misunderstanding of research that showed that puppies must have contact with people beginning no later than the 49th day or they will not bond well with people later in life. It doesn't matter who the people are, only that they are human beings who treat the puppy with kindness. In fact, the end of the seventh week is the absolute earliest that a puppy should leave his mother and siblings, but it is not necessarily the best time for a new home. Many puppies benefit from another one to nine weeks with their natal families if the environment is healthful and stimulating. If you want a well-adjusted dog, do not purchase or adopt one who has been isolated from human contact from 7 to 16 weeks of age. If you already have the young puppy, be sure to socialize him well from 7 to 16 weeks. (We will talk more about socialization later in this chapter.)

Another important factor must be considered when deciding the best time to take your puppy home. At some time around eight to ten weeks of age, most puppies go through the first and most severe of several fear imprint periods (or just fear periods). (Many puppies experience milder fear periods around 9 and 18 months of age, although some pups never seem to notice.) This eight-week fear period is linked to the rapid-learning developmental period that occurs during a puppy's seventh and eighth weeks and is part of a dog's heritage as a wild predator who had to learn quickly or die. When he is going though a fear period, a puppy is especially prone to being frightened by a variety of things. Sights and sounds that he didn't seem to notice the week before may suddenly terrify him, and unusual events or painful experiences can cause emotional trauma that may lead to problem behaviors for a very long time. It's important to shield the puppy as much as possible from potentially scary experiences during the fear period, including

*Young puppies learn quickly, and the lessons they learn can last a lifetime.*

a move to a new home, visits to the veterinarian, and so forth.

If you devote time to your puppy from his 49th to 56th day, you can establish a foundation that will last a lifetime. You and your pup can forge a bond that will grow richer over time. You also can use short, positive training sessions to teach him some basic commands and behaviors that you will refine later. More importantly, you can teach him how to learn and enjoy the process. The downside of this ability to learn at lightning speed is that the puppy will remember bad experiences as well as good. Therefore, any training you do during fear periods should be especially gentle and completely positive, and the puppy should be sheltered as much as possible from things that may frighten him.

## PREPARING YOUR PUPPY TO LEARN

Many people think that puppy training shouldn't begin until the puppy is six months old. As we have already seen, though, puppies are little information sponges, ready and eager to learn about the world and how to live in it. So don't wait—begin training your puppy as soon as you bring him home. By the time he's six months

*Your puppy should begin learning what you want him to do from the time you bring him home—with plenty of time for sleep, of course.*

old, he will have learned a lot, and I promise you will be happier if he learns what you want him to know so that you won't have to "unlearn" him later.

This section will show you how to help your puppy learn by following a few basic steps.

## Integrate Training Into Your Routine

Training can and should be integrated into daily life. Use routine events—like puppy dinnertime, playtime, and going for a walk—as opportunities to teach and reinforce basic commands and behaviors. Your puppy will quickly learn to come when called, sit and lie down on command, potty outdoors, and so forth if you reward him with his dinner, a walk, a tummy rub, or playtime. Popular movies and television shows to the contrary, dogs don't come preprogrammed to behave according to human rules. They do, luckily, come preprogrammed to learn, and thousands of years of domestication equip them perfectly to live with us in harmony and love. If you teach your puppy what you want him to know and do, he will make you the happiest dog owner in town.

## Keep Training Sessions Short

As you begin your puppy's education, remember that the younger he is, the shorter his attention span. Keep "formal" training sessions short, make them fun, repeat them frequently, and focus on just one behavior each session. If you spend two minutes several times a day teaching your puppy sit or down or come, he will learn quickly, and the process will be more fun for both of you. If your puppy does what you ask two or three times, quit for a while and play with him. Even when he is grown up and able to focus longer, play breaks should remain a part of training.

## Be Consistent

Your puppy will learn more quickly if all human members of your household follow the same puppy rules and use the same training techniques. Dogs can and do sort out who's who—the soft touch, the one-who-must-be-obeyed—but they learn more quickly with consistency. If you like to cuddle your puppy on the couch, but your spouse tells him to stay off the furniture, the pup will be confused (and your spouse will be frustrated). Be forewarned—people are a lot harder to train than puppies are!

## Prevent Bad Habits From Forming

Behaviors that your puppy repeats more than a few times become habits, and as we all know, it's hard to break a bad habit. You can make puppy raising much easier for yourself if you prevent bad habits, and the easiest way to do that is to:

- **Supervise.** Make sure that your puppy is supervised when he's

### Toy Safety and Rotation

If you're like most puppy owners, your canine baby has a mountain of toys to play with. That's fine, but two cautions:

1. **Be sure that the toys are safe.** Your puppy's toys should be too big to swallow and free of plastic eyes, squeakers, ribbons, or other parts that might hurt him. You'd be amazed at the things puppies will swallow—like socks, hand towels, and rope—so check all toys frequently, and remove any that have become dangerous.

2. **Rotate the toys.** If your puppy has 30 toys strewn across the floor all the time, he may lose interest in them, making him more likely to gnaw on your shoes or chair legs—not to mention the hazard to your own health if you trip over a woobie or step barefoot on a chew bone. A better approach is to rotate the toys. Give your puppy two or three toys at a time, including something good for chewing and something good for shaking and "killing." Switch toys every few days. Your puppy will be thrilled to see his "old friends" and won't become bored.

*Your puppy is eager to learn, so be patient with him, and make training fun.*

loose in your house or yard and safely confined when he can't be supervised. If you leave your puppy alone in your house for a half hour, you're the one who needs a spanking if he piddles on the Persian carpet and chews a hole in your great-grandma's quilt.

- **Be proactive.** If your puppy hasn't learned to come when you call him, don't let him loose outside without a leash and then get angry if he doesn't come when you call him. If he isn't yet housetrained, don't give him the run of the house and then get angry when he piddles on the carpet.

- **Plan ahead.** Even if your puppy is still a little round furball, think ahead to the adolescent and adult he will become and the behavior you will expect from that animal. If you don't want your 70-pound (31.8-kg) retriever to nap on the couch, don't lift him up beside you when he's a cuddly 10 pounds (4.5 kg). If you don't want him to hop onto the kitchen counter when his legs are long enough for the leap, don't groom him on the counter when he's a baby. And as tempting as it is to spoil your puppy, remember that it will be easier to loosen the rules as he matures and becomes more trustworthy than it will be to tighten the rules after he forms habits you don't like.

- **Focus on the positive, forget the negative.** It's very difficult to learn to do nothing. Your puppy will learn what you don't want more quickly if you give him an acceptable alternative. Don't just scream and scold when he nibbles your new designer shoes. (Who left them where the puppy could get them, anyway?) Do gently take the shoe away, give him a chew toy, and when he sinks his little teeth into that, praise him for being a good puppy. Then close your closet.

## Be Patient

Don't expect your puppy to learn everything in a week or two. Learning new things is hard work and takes time. But if you approach puppy training with love, patience, consistency, willingness to learn, and a sense of humor, you will build a solid relationship with a well-mannered, confident dog.

## Make Training Fun

As you prepare to train your puppy, remember that this should be fun! Maybe not every minute of every training session will be enjoyable, but for the most part you and your pup should enjoy all aspects of living together, including training. Your goal shouldn't be simply to make your dog obey you. It should be to build a relationship based on mutual learning, love, trust, and understanding so that he will want to do what you ask, not out of fear or obligation but out of a desire to please you and be rewarded.

*Puppies must meet all kinds of people if they are to develop into confident, social adult dogs.*

## Double Trouble

Are you thinking that two puppies will be double the fun? Maybe—but they will almost certainly also be more than double the trouble unless you make an extra effort to raise them right. Puppies who grow up together, especially littermates, often bond closely to one another and less closely to people. Raising two together also may complicate socialization, housetraining, and other training.

If you really must raise two (or more!) puppies at the same time, you must give each of them individual time and training for at least the first 18 months. Let them play together two or three times a day for an hour or so, but don't keep them together all the time unless you want them to bond more strongly to one another than to you and to be completely dependent on one another. To mature into a healthy, confident adult, each puppy needs to learn to function without the other. He needs to spend time alone with his toys, and he needs one-on-one play and training time with his person or people.

If you want two dogs of about the same age, consider starting with one. Give him a good start, and when he's about 9 to 18 months old, bring home a second puppy. Or better yet—adopt a second young (or older) adult from a rescue organization or shelter. And think carefully about having dogs close to the same age—they not only live together, but they grow old and often die around the same time. I speak from experience when I say it isn't easy to lose multiple old dogs within a short period of time.

# SOCIALIZATION

Socialization—the process of introducing your puppy to the world around him—is essential to his emotional and behavioral development. Although the socialization process should continue at least through the first two years of your dog's life, it is especially critical between the 7th and 16th weeks. (However, special care should be taken and socialization possibly halted during the fear-imprint period.) This is so important because a dog who is not socialized as a puppy is likely to become a dog who is afraid of the unfamiliar. Some fearful dogs respond by cowering, hiding, running or trying to run away, or by displaying extremely submissive behavior, such as urination, in inappropriate situations. Such behaviors can be hard to live with and hard to fix, but they don't hurt anyone except the unhappy dog. More serious, though, are the "fear biters," dogs who respond to their fear and anxiety with aggression. Fear biters are very dangerous because they are unpredictable.

## How To Socialize Your Dog

Because puppies are at our mercy for their social life, it is our responsibility to take the time necessary to socialize them. We have to do this particularly during those critical 7th through 16th weeks, which are the developmental window of opportunity for canine socialization, but the process should continue throughout puberty and young adulthood.

*To become properly socialized, your dog needs to meet all kinds of people, see different types of places, and experience a variety of surfaces under his feet.*

## People, Places, and Things

To become properly socialized, your puppy needs to meet all kinds of people: babies, toddlers, children, teenagers, old people, young adults, women, men, people of different races, clean-shaven people, bearded people, long-haired people, bald people—you get the picture. He also needs to see different kinds of places—parks, city sidewalks, quiet places, noisy places. He needs to experience a variety of surfaces under his feet—concrete, grass, gravel, dirt, carpet, vinyl, wooden walkways. Exposing your dog to a wide variety of people, places, and things will make him more confident and comfortable throughout his life, whether he's in familiar surroundings or a new setting. Just be sure to keep him away from public places that might be frequented by sick or unvaccinated dogs. If you are uncertain about a particular place, ask your vet how to balance the need to socialize your puppy with the need to protect him from contagious diseases.

Once your puppy has received all his puppy vaccinations, your options expand. You can take him to parks, playgrounds, different neighborhoods, outdoor shopping centers (and a few stores that allow dogs), the sidewalk outside stores—wherever he will meet new people and see new things. Your puppy should always be on leash in public. For one thing, it's the law in many places. For another, a leash keeps your puppy safe and helps the people you meet feel more comfortable. (It's difficult to believe, but there are people who don't want to meet your puppy!)

### Other Dogs

Your puppy also must meet and interact with other dogs. He cannot develop proper doggy social skills or learn to communicate effectively with others of his species if he grows up without canine contact. Of course, a young puppy is vulnerable to both injury and infectious disease, so you need to use good judgment about the dogs your puppy meets. Once again, remember that he is vulnerable to common canine diseases until he is fully vaccinated, so avoid high-risk environments where urine or feces from other dogs may expose your puppy to bacteria, viruses, or parasites. Also, be alert and exercise caution, especially when encountering dogs you don't know. Most adult dogs will tolerate a rowdy puppy or discipline him gently, but just one lightning-fast encounter with the wrong dog could leave your puppy frightened or badly injured.

Socialization can begin at home if you have an adult dog or

**Safety for Puppies in Training**

If you plan eventually to participate with your puppy in athletic events, keep in mind that his immature body is vulnerable to injury that can cause permanent damage. Although no puppy should be pushed too quickly in training, this is especially important for the larger breeds, for whom growth is a longer process. Their young bodies are not ready for exercise that causes sharp or repetitive impact during the first year—longer in large and giant breeds.

High-impact and leg-twisting activities, such as leaping in the air to catch flying objects, weaving through weave poles, jogging or running (especially on hard surfaces), and repetitive jumping should be postponed until you are sure that your puppy's growth plates are closed. You can make an educated guess about when the growth plates will close if you know approximately how big your dog will be at maturity (9 to 10 months for a dog of 25 pounds [11.3 kg] or less; at least 14 months for a medium to large dog of 25 to 100 pounds [11.3 kg to 45.4 kg]; at least 18 months for a giant dog of 100 pounds [45.4 kg] or more).

It is also possible to have your vet X-ray your puppy to see whether the growth plates are open or closed. Many people are in a hurry to begin competing with their young dogs, but don't sacrifice your pup's safety to impatience—waiting just a few months can make a lifetime of difference for your dog.

two. If you have friends with healthy, good-natured adult dogs whom you know are properly vaccinated and tolerant of puppies, you might invite them over (one at a time) for a little playtime. Puppies must learn to understand warnings from adult dogs, and it's not fair to expect an adult to put up with unlimited puppy antics or to expose a puppy to possible injury from a fed-up adult. Young puppies can be extremely annoying, and those needle-sharp teeth can try even the most patient of canine uncles and aunties. Even mother dogs find their puppies obnoxious

at times! So supervise all interaction between your puppy and other dogs for the first few weeks, and don't let things get out of control. Do not leave them alone together no matter how well things seem to be going, and if the older dog's patience is wearing thin, give him a break.

### Other Animals

Your puppy also should have the opportunity to meet other animals that he may encounter in his travels through life. If you have cats or other small pets, introduce them to your puppy slowly and carefully. An exuberant puppy can injure a smaller animal without meaning to, and if your dog has a strong prey drive (the urge to hunt), he may see the other animal as legitimate prey. Know your puppy's breed—some dogs (particularly terriers and hounds) are instinctive hunters. If yours is, be very cautious about letting him have access to other pets, and do not allow him to chase or attack them from the start.

## CRATE TRAINING

Using a crate will make raising your puppy a lot easier for you and safer for him. He doesn't yet know what he's allowed to do and what's safe and unsafe. He can't control the urge to potty when it comes upon him. In short, he doesn't need to be loose unsupervised. Never use a crate to punish your puppy, and don't shove him in or yell as you put him there. His crate should be a good, safe place, and he should enter it willingly.

## Crate Size

If your puppy is young, an adult-sized crate will be much more room than he needs—which is not a problem unless he decides to potty at one end of the crate and sleep at the other. In that case, until he's housetrained, block off part of the crate or use a smaller one until he is either trained or too big for the smaller space. The reason that crates work so well for housetraining is that most dogs don't like to sleep where they potty, so until he is reliable about not eliminating in his crate, your puppy should have only enough room to stand up, turn around, and lie down. (For information on what types of crates are available, see Chapter 4.)

## Crate Accessories

As mentioned in Chapter 4, you may or may not want to use a liner or crate pad with a puppy. If yours is a chewer or ripper-upper, leave the padding out until he outgrows that behavior. Padding also can prolong housetraining because it absorbs accidents, making them less unpleasant for the puppy to live with. Some people put newspaper in puppy crates, but if your puppy has ever been placed on newspaper to potty, it may confuse the training issue, making him think that the crate is the right place to do his business. Newspaper also imparts a rather yucky odor to puppies, especially if it gets damp. The sweet musky smell of a clean puppy is much nicer. Whatever you do, don't line your puppy's crate with wee-wee pads—plastic-lined paper pads impregnated with a hormone that tells the puppy "potty here."

*Feeding your puppy in the crate will help him to associate it with good things.*

## Duration of Confinement

How long should a puppy stay in a crate? The general guideline for most breeds is the puppy's age plus one. So if your puppy is two months old, he can probably be crated without having an

*Crate training is an excellent way to keep your puppy safe and out of mischief when you can't supervise him.*

accident for up to three hours. If he's six months old, up to seven hours. But remember, every puppy is an individual, and toy-breed and other small puppies may need to go out much more often than that. If your four-month-old pup can "hold it" for three hours but piddles at three and a half, you'll have to find a way to get him out to potty every three hours. And remember, it's unfair and unkind to keep any dog crated regularly for more than four hours at a time. (Most adult dogs can occasionally tolerate crating for eight or nine hours under unusual circumstances, but that's hard on a dog physically and mentally and should not be an everyday occurrence. How would you like to stay in one small room with no toilet for eight hours?)

## How to Crate Train Your Dog

To crate train your dog, follow these steps:

1. Don't place your puppy's crate in an isolated area. He should be in a well-traveled part of the house so that he's surrounded by your smell even when you aren't there.

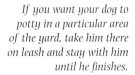

*If you want your dog to potty in a particular area of the yard, take him there on leash and stay with him until he finishes.*

2. Feed your puppy in his crate, and teach him to enter at other times by tossing in a treat or a special chew toy as you say "Crate!" or "Kennel!"

3. Praise him when he gets in.

4. Leave the crate door open when your puppy is playing outside it so that he can go in and out when he wants to. My adult dogs still get into their crates voluntarily and nap there with the doors wide open.

5. Don't always close the door when your puppy goes in, and when you do close it, give him another small treat.

6. Close your puppy into the crate for varying amounts of time—obviously sometimes he'll be there for an hour or two when you have to leave or at night, but another time it may be only a few seconds or a few minutes. This way, your puppy won't associate the crate strictly with long periods without you.

7. Don't make a fuss when you let him out. Freedom is its own reward, and you don't want to plant or reinforce the idea that being in the crate is bad and being out of the crate is good.

8. If you have other pets who are not crated when you leave, put your puppy's crate near where they tend to spend time. If you crate your other dogs when you're gone, put the crates near one

another. Your puppy won't feel so alone.

9. If possible, put the crate in your bedroom at night so that your puppy doesn't feel isolated from his "pack" and so that you can hear him if he needs to be let out to potty during the night.

10. When you need to confine your puppy, make getting into the crate a good thing—use a happy voice, and reward him with a treat or safe chew toy.

# HOUSETRAINING

Most people agree that one of the first and most important things a puppy needs to learn is where to potty. In fact, lack of reliable housetraining, or knowing when and where not to potty, is one of the leading reasons that dogs are turned into shelters or dumped by their owners. Barring a physical problem or serious mental quirk, most dogs can learn not to eliminate in the house, but some require more diligent training over several months. Some breeds tend to be easier to housetrain than others, but it's essential

*When housetraining, confine your puppy to rooms with washable flooring so that mistakes don't ruin carpets.*

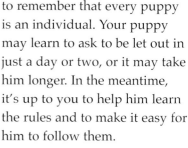

to remember that every puppy is an individual. Your puppy may learn to ask to be let out in just a day or two, or it may take him longer. In the meantime, it's up to you to help him learn the rules and to make it easy for him to follow them.

Healthy puppies raised in a clean environment usually like to be clean. But a puppy cannot control his bladder or bowels until he is several months old. It's your job to anticipate his needs. Typically, puppies need to urinate and defecate shortly after they wake up, during or shortly after a meal, and

*You can teach your dog to potty on command by giving him a cue to go and giving him a treat when he finishes.*

during or after exercise. Some puppies can go an hour between potty breaks, but others—especially toy breeds and other tiny pups—need to go much more often. It makes sense that tiny little organs have tiny little capacities. If you have to take your puppy to his "potty" every ten minutes when he's up and active, then that's what you have to do. You will undoubtedly make some potty runs in the wee hours of the morning for the first few weeks, too.

## How to Housetrain Your Dog

To housetrain your dog, follow these steps:

1. Whenever your puppy is loose in the house, watch him closely. If he begins to sniff around, circle, or arch his back, pick him up and take him out immediately. Don't expect him to walk out the

### Litter and Paper Training

Some people with tiny toy dogs like to teach them to use an indoor litter pan or eliminate on newspaper. Use the same general method to litter or paper train your dog, except you probably don't need a leash, and obviously you don't need to go out the door. I would recommend litter or paper training only if you intend to use these methods, at least part of the time, throughout your dog's life (not a bad idea if you live in an upstairs apartment with a tiny dog). But if you want your dog eventually to eliminate outdoors only, then train him to do that right from the start. Forget litter and paper training—you'll end up having to retrain later.

door—he may not have the physical control necessary to make it that far. As he matures and develops control, you won't have to carry him (which is good if he's a growing into a big dog).

2. If you want your dog to learn to use a particular part of the yard, take him there on leash and stay with him until he finishes, then praise him in a happy voice and give him a small treat on occasion. (Don't play with him until he's finished eliminating—keep him focused on the job at hand.) He will form the habit of going there and nowhere else in the yard, especially if you keep the area clear of feces.

3. Teach your pup to go "on command." When he begins to go, tell him "Go potty" or "Hurry up," and give him a little treat when he finishes. Do this consistently for a while, and soon he will associate the words with the act of eliminating. You'll be able to take him out, say your command, and he'll do the job in a jiffy!

4. If your puppy doesn't go within 10 minutes, take him inside and put him in his crate for 10 to 15 minutes, then take him to potty again. When he does go, praise him and reward him. That's the time to play a little, too. Wait a few minutes before you take him in—he may not have completely emptied his bladder or bowels on the first attempt.

Even if you don't care where in the yard your dog goes, I'd recommend taking him on leash to potty at least part of the time so that he learns that he can go with a leash attached. By the same token, when he is safely vaccinated, take him to other places so that he learns he doesn't have to be home to potty. Be sure to take plastic clean-up bags so that you can clean up after your pup. If your dog thinks he can go only off-leash in his own backyard, he may have a serious problem if you take him somewhere for the weekend.

Depending on his breed and his individual traits, your puppy may be housetrained in a couple of weeks or not for several months. Even if he's not completely reliable, though, he should show signs of progress by the time he's four or five months old. If he is still having regular accidents in the house at six months or older, speak to your veterinarian to be sure that your dog doesn't have a medical problem.

## Dealing With Accidents

Be prepared for a few accidents, and do not punish your puppy if he has one. Punishment (nose rubbing, hitting, yelling) won't help your puppy learn what you want him to do, and he may fear that every time you see him potty you're going to punish him. You may think that the obvious solution is for him to go outdoors, but your puppy doesn't know that dogs are supposed to pee and poop outdoors. He may think you don't want him to go at all, but of course he has to, and he may believe that his only option is to go potty where you can't see him. This may make for a long-term problem if he starts hiding behind the furniture to do his business.

If you see your puppy pottying in the house, or if he acts like he needs to, calmly pick him up and take him outside. (Being picked up nearly always makes the puppy stop, and having something left to do outside will make the lesson more clear to him.) When he finishes in the correct place, praise him and give him a treat if you have one with you. Take him back in and put him in his crate or in a safe, confined area while you clean up. Clean the spot with a good odor and stain remover made for organic waste—you can find several such products in pet supply stores. A cheap alternative to neutralize urine (but not feces) is a 50/50 mixture of white vinegar and water. It's critical that you remove all the odor, and household cleansers won't do that. (Even if you can't smell urine or feces, your puppy might be able to. Remember, even a young puppy interprets the world largely through what he smells, and the smell of urine or feces tells him "Potty here.") If your puppy isn't completely housetrained, don't let him leave the room where you are, and don't leave him unsupervised.

Can you go eight or nine hours without a potty break? It's easy to see that asking a puppy to wait that long is unfair and unrealistic, so make arrangements for your pup to get breaks even if you have to work. If you can't come home and take him out at

*If you see your puppy pottying in the house, calmly pick him up and take him outside to finish.*

lunchtime, consider hiring a pet sitter or other reliable person to come in once or twice during the day to walk him, play with him, and if necessary, feed him. Your puppy will be happier and will be housetrained more quickly, and you won't have quite as much puppy energy to manage when you do get home. If money is an issue, maybe you can exchange services with a friend or neighbor.

Here are a few more suggestions to make housetraining accidents less likely:

- If you plan to purchase a puppy, buy from a responsible breeder who has kept the puppy in clean surroundings and who has already started potty training.
- Confine your puppy, preferably to a crate, when you can't watch him.
- If possible, confine your puppy to rooms with washable flooring so that mistakes don't ruin carpets.
- Feed your puppy a high-quality dry dog food—it will keep his stools more solid, making self-control easier. Feed him at least four hours before bedtime.
- If he eats dry dog food, your pup will need plenty of water. However, until he is fully housetrained, remove water two hours before bedtime.
- Keep your puppy on a schedule—try to feed and exercise him at the same time every day while he's being potty trained.

## PUPPY KINDERGARTEN

You will do most of your puppy training at home, of course, but a good puppy kindergarten class will give both of you several advantages. Puppy classes usually meet once a week for four to eight weeks and usually last 30 to 60 minutes a session. Classes help with socialization because your puppy interacts with other puppies and with people. Your commitment to a class schedule ensures that you do at least that much training, and homework encourages you to keep it up for at least a few minutes every day. After all, you want your puppy to be an honor student, don't you? Puppy kindergarten also gives you a head start on later training, and an experienced, well-qualified instructor will help you find the most effective methods for your puppy and guide you when you don't know what to do next. She also should address home training issues and other aspects of puppy raising.

Rough training methods are bad for any dog, but for a puppy, they can be devastating. Positive, reward-based training gets much better results and builds a deep and lasting relationship between dog and human, so look for an instructor and class that use a positive, motivational approach to training. (See Chapter 5.) Your puppy is a baby, and he will make mistakes. When he does, he must be guided to the correct behavior and rewarded when he gets it right.

Training should be a form of play, not an ordeal, so keep it interesting, varied, and fun for both of you—not just when your dog is a puppy but all through his life.

*Puppies start learning early, even before they leave their mother and siblings.*

# Chapter 7

# BASIC TRAINING

Even if you have no interest in advanced training of any kind, a basic education will make your dog a better-behaved, more confident companion and make you a happier dog owner. If you started with a puppy and worked through the puppy training and socialization covered in the last chapter, you're ready to continue his education with the basic training skills in this chapter. If you're starting out with an adult dog who missed puppy training or whose background you don't know, you might want to review the information in Chapter 6 and then proceed. Either way, get your dog and let's start training and learning!

## THE RECALL (COME)

A reliable *recall*—meaning your dog comes to you when you call or signal—is one of the most important trained behaviors he can learn. First of all, responding promptly to your call could save his life someday. And let's face it, you will save yourself a lot of frustration if your dog comes when you want him. But how many dogs do you know who come reliably when their owners call them? By calling their dogs without taking the time to teach them to respond correctly, most people actually teach their dogs that they don't have to come when called. If you follow the plan outlined here, your dog will understand that he must come when you call, and he will want to do so.

### Before You Begin

Before you begin teaching the *recall*, I'm going to suggest a few things that you can do to increase your chances of success. First, if you don't yet have your dog, now is the time to set the stage for teaching him to come every time you call. Plan for success, and when your new puppy or dog joins your life, follow the guidelines and avoid the potential pitfalls right from the start.

If you have an adult dog, you've probably already tried to teach him to come when you call. If he's reliable most of the time, great—use the information here to reinforce what he has already learned and to improve his performance. But if he's not exactly spot-on when you holler out the door, you need to rethink your strategy and start over.

*A basic education will make your dog better behaved and more confident.*

This training will go more smoothly if you treat the *recall* as a new behavior you are teaching rather than as a faulty one you're repairing.

To make it "new," find a different word to use to call your dog. If you've been yelling "Come" while your dog continues to sniff the bunny trails in the yard, start over with "Here." Your dog ignores "Come," but he has not learned to ignore "Here." The hardest part will be retraining yourself to use the right word.

Remember the six principles of successful training that we discussed in Chapter 5? Let's see how they apply to the *recall*.

1. **Be consistent.** Always use the same word to call your dog. If you play the obedience lottery with different words like "come," "come here," "here," "get over here," or "get your butt over here," you will probably lose more often than you win.

2. **Be concise.** Do not call more than once unless you want to teach your dog to ignore you. If he doesn't come when you call, go back as many steps in training as you need to. Be patient! A reliable *recall* is not learned or taught overnight.

3. **Be generous.** Reward your dog every time he comes when called. At first, the rewards should be big ones—a special treat, a jackpot sometimes. Eventually, you can scale back to an ear scratch and praise, with intermittent treats.

4. **Be smart.** Never, ever let your dog off his leash in an unfenced area if he doesn't come every single time you call him, despite the squirrels square dancing nearby. Even if you think he's reliable, be extremely cautious. I know of more than one very obedient dog who was killed the one and only time he didn't come when called.

5. **Be prepared.** Until your dog is very, very reliable, don't call him if you are not in a position to enforce the command. If you aren't sure he will come when you call him, put him on a leash or long line before he goes out in the rain so that you can get him back in.

6. **Be happy.** Never call your dog to you in anger or to do something to him that he won't like. If you need to put drops in his ears or put him in his crate for a while, go get him instead of calling him. Coming to you should always be safe and wonderful for your dog.

As with many behaviors, you can use a combination of techniques that we discussed in Chapter 5 to teach and reinforce the *recall*. You can use capturing and shaping techniques (the simplest method) to reinforce your dog's natural inclination to come to you, or you can lure him.

## Teaching *Recall* Step by Step

### *Capturing and Shaping*

1. Carry treats or part of your dog's daily kibble allotment. When your dog comes to you without any prompting, mark that behavior and reward him, sometimes with a treat, sometimes with a belly rub or ear massage.

2. After you have done this a number of times, your dog will probably begin to check in with you regularly. When he's on his

*Begin teaching the recall with your dog on leash, and always reward him for coming when you call him.*

way to you and appears to be committed, you can begin to use your cue word: "Rowdy, come!"

3. If your dog tends to stop and sniff or travel a zigzag path to get to you, don't call him—just continue to reward him when he gets to you on his own. If you add the cue when your dog is not performing reliably, you simply teach him to ignore the word. But the rewards—treats, play, scratches—still reinforce the idea that coming to you is a good thing.

### Luring

1. Begin with your puppy or dog on leash or in a small fenced area or room where he can't get too far from you. In a happy voice, say "Rowdy, come!" Then act silly, walk or run the other way, or crouch down—whatever you need to do to make your dog curious and encourage him to come to you.

2. When you start, mark his first steps toward you with your

# TROUBLESHOOTING
## The *Recall*

### Rowdy *ignores you when you call him.*

I've said it before, but it's worth repeating: If you repeatedly call your dog when he doesn't come, you teach him to ignore the command. Whether his failure to respond is due to lack of training or to some irresistible distraction in his environment makes no difference—either way, he needs to learn (or relearn) that he must come when you call him. Put him back on his leash or longline, and train him.

### Rowdy *doesn't reliably* come *on command.*

Again, unless your dog comes every single time you call, you need to put him back on his leash or longline and repeat the training steps. Also, know that even the most reliable dog can have a momentary lapse in obedience. Some dogs, because of the drives they are born with, should never, ever be off leash in an unfenced area. This is particularly true of hounds, terriers, and some working and sporting dogs, but any dog can get squirrelitis and run into a street.

### Rowdy *doesn't come, despite your best efforts.*

Put a leash or longline on him. Call him once, then gently pull him in your direction. If he moves toward you on his own, stop pulling, encourage him with happy talk, and reward him when he gets to you. Then let him do what he wants (within reason!), but keep the leash on as long as you are practicing *recalls*. In addition, be smart—if you take your dog out to potty, put a leash or longline on him so that you can get him back. Don't give your dog a chance to make a mistake.

marker. As he learns to respond reliably to the *recall* cue, wait until he's closer to you to mark his behavior so that eventually you use the marker only when he's within reach of you.

3. Reward him after you mark his movement toward you—give him a treat, play with him, whatever makes him happy. Then let him go back to what he was doing—you don't want him to associate responding to the *recall* with the end of his fun.

4. Repeat the process two or three times, then quit for this session. Practice *recalls* several times a day, and use "real life" opportunities such as doggy dinner time to reinforce the command.

You can make a game of teaching the *recall* by having household members stand in a circle, calling your dog back and forth and rewarding him. Just make sure that only one person calls at a time.

## SIT

The *sit*—meaning "put your tail end on the ground"—is a useful command in many situations. For one thing, it gives you a means of telling your dog to control himself when he's excited or when you're out and about meeting neighbors, watching cars and bicycles go by, or visiting the vet. The *sit* also provides an alternative behavior when your rambunctious pooch is doing something you don't want him to do. By telling him to sit when you think he is about to do something you don't like, you turn a negative behavior to a positive one and reinforce him for being a "good dog." A dog who understands the *sit* command also can be reassured in stressful situations—if you tell him to sit, he knows that you're in control of the situation and

*Sit is a useful command that all dogs should learn.*

Nag, nag, nag. Do you listen carefully to people who nag you? Neither will your dog. If you repeat a command over and over but you don't teach your dog what it means—and that he really does have to do it—he'll tune you out. So don't say "Sit sit sit sit sit" and then go on to something else while your dog continues sniffing the floor. Say "Sit," and if he doesn't, calmly put his leash on and have a short *sit* training session.

he's relieved of having to make a decision or take action. If you plan to compete with your dog in obedience, rally, or agility, nice quick *sits* are indispensable.

If you're like most dog owners, you're probably thinking, "Oh, Rowdy already knows how to sit on command. He always sits for his dinner." Good for Rowdy! But does he remain sitting until you release him? Does he sit on command no matter where he is or what's happening around him? Does he sit when you tell him just once? Many pet dogs will sit for a second or two, often for food or a tennis ball toss, then pop right back up and resume whatever they were doing before. That's a start, but if Rowdy won't sit the first time you tell him no matter what and stay sitting until you release him, he isn't really trained to sit on command. This section will show you how to get a reliable *sit* every time.

## Before You Start

You can capture your dog's spontaneous *sits* by marking and rewarding them, or you can shape the *sit* by marking and rewarding closer and closer approximations of a complete *sit* (see Chapter 5), but those techniques take time, especially if your dog is not yet very familiar with the "mark-and-treat" game. You also could try to model the *sit* by pushing down on your dog's hips to force him into position, but I don't recommend that for a couple of reasons. First, if you position your dog, he doesn't develop the reaction to the command and the muscle memory that enables him eventually to respond automatically. He may learn to rely on the physical signal of your hand on his posterior rather than the verbal command, or if you teach one, a hand signal. Another reason I don't recommend butt pushing is that your dog's natural response to pressure is to exert his own pressure in the opposite direction. You push, he pushes back. You pull, he pulls back. Why have a shoving contest when you can work together? Worse still, you could injure your dog's spine or hips by pushing down on them.

Luring, on the other hand, is a good technique for teaching the *sit* command.

## Teaching *Sit* Step by Step

1. Begin with your dog on leash or confined in a small space. Hold a treat in front of his nose, but don't let him take it.
2. Slowly raise the treat enough to clear the top of his head, and

move it back over his head toward his tail. The laws of physics will take over, and as his head comes up to keep track of the treat, his fanny will approach the ground.

3. As your dog folds his hind legs to sit, tell him "Sit." When his rear end is on the floor, mark and give him the treat. Then release him.

4. Repeat this exercise three or four times per session.

A sloppy *sit*, in which your dog rolls one hip sideways instead of sitting squarely on his "butt bones," is probably no big deal for most pets. But if you plan to train your dog for competition, it's a good idea to insist on nice square *sits* from the start. To teach your

# TROUBLESHOOTING
## The *Sit*

### Rowdy likes the lure but doesn't raise his head to follow it.

Keep your hand closer to his nose, and move it more slowly. Close your hand over the treat if he tries to snatch it.

### Rowdy jumps up to get the treat.

Jumping up usually means that you're holding the treat too high. Keep it closer to your dog's head, but don't let him have it until he sits. If he gets really pushy about it, make the treat "disappear" by raising it completely out of his reach or by putting it behind your back until he settles down. He'll soon learn that being too pushy makes the treat go away.

### Rowdy raises his head but not enough to make his back legs fold into a sit. He just doesn't seem to get it.

Continue to hold the treat near his nose. As you slowly raise the treat and move it toward his tail, cradle the curve of his hind legs with your other arm and gently fold him into a *sit*. (Your arm should be above the hock joint, which is the sharp angle above the long bone above his rear paw.) When his fanny is on the floor, mark and give him the treat. Most dogs get the idea with this gentle modeling without becoming dependent on it.

### Rowdy doesn't come, despite your best efforts.

Put a leash or longline on him. Call him once, then gently pull him in your direction. If he moves toward you on his own, stop pulling, encourage him with happy talk, and reward him when he gets to you. Then let him do what he wants (within reason!), but keep the leash on as long as you are practicing recalls. In addition, be smart—if you take your dog out to potty, put a leash or long line on him so that you can get him back. Don't give your dog a chance to make a mistake.

### Rowdy steps backward instead of sitting.

Put his leash on and hold it so that he can't back up. (Don't pull him forward, just keep him from backing up.)

### Rowdy sits squarely at first but then rolls to one hip.

Mark and reward him only when he sits properly. If he slides into a sloppy *sit*, use your lure to encourage him back into a square *sit*, and then mark and reward. Be sure that you mark, reward, and release him only when he is sitting properly.

dog that "sit" means "sit squarely on your butt," be sure to mark and reward only nice, square *sits*. That way, your dog will learn that the only position that counts for this command is the straight, square *sit*.

As your dog learns to respond reliably to the *sit* command, you can up the ante if you want to. Reward him only for faster and faster responses. Have him hold the *sit* longer before you reward him. (Later in this chapter, we'll work on the *stay* command; but even without telling him to stay, your dog should continue doing what you told him until you release him.)

## SETTLE

*Settle* is the command I use to mean "lie down from a *sit*, and roll onto one hip." This is a basic control command that differs from my more advanced *down* command (see Chapter 8), which calls for a dog to lie down in the sphinx position, or a "fold-back drop," from a standing or moving position. When your dog rolls onto one hip with the *settle* command, he is in a more relaxed position and will have to work harder to get up again, unlike with the *down*, which puts him in a position to pop right back up.

The *settle* command should be part of every dog's training vocabulary. Being able to have your dog lie down from a *sit* and stay there can be a matter of convenience as well as safety—who needs a dog underfoot when you're carrying hot dishes to the table? Also, he will need to know how to settle if you plan to train or compete in obedience or to teach him to be a therapy dog.

*The command to settle, or lie down, is one of the most useful things your dog can learn.*

### Before You Start

Lying down on command may seem pretty basic, but like the *recall*, a lot of dogs never learn the

Be sure to mark and reward the behavior you want your dog to repeat. He will associate the marker and reward with whatever immediately precedes them. So if you want to teach him to sit, at first you must mark within a split second of the moment his fanny hits the floor. Then, slowly, over the course of many repetitions, wait until he has kept it there for a longer and longer time. If you are slow and don't mark until after he sits and then stands and wags his tail at you, he will associate the marker and the reward with standing and wagging or even with the sequence sit|stand|wag.

command well enough to be reliable. This is partly because of the nature of the *settle* position itself. Remember in Chapter 2 when we talked about dominance and submission and the signals that indicate submission? One of those signals is lying down. Because being down on the ground indicates submission and therefore vulnerability, some dogs resist assuming that position, especially in situations where other dogs are present. If your dog seems to be nervous about putting himself in a vulnerable or submissive position, move him away from the other dogs and try again. Find a distance at which he is less resistant, and slowly (over the course of several training sessions) have him lie down closer to the group until he's part of it.

Another factor that can affect how well your dog learns the *settle* command is lack of consistency. That principle of training is essential, but you need to use the right word all the time if you want your dog to perform the correct command consistently. So use "settle" if you want him to lie down and make himself comfortable when he is sitting and "down" when you want him to drop to the ground from a standing or moving position.

We'll teach the *settle* command by luring your dog into position.

## Teaching *Settle* Step by Step

1. To teach the *settle* command, first teach your dog to sit on command. (See section "Sit.")
2. When he is sitting, lure him down with a treat in your hand. If he automatically rolls onto one hip, mark and reward him with the treat. If he lowers his front end but remains in the sphinx position with both hips upright, gently roll him onto one hip, then mark and reward him.
3. As your dog understands the *settle* command, you will be able to skip the *sit* command and simply tell him to settle. Some dogs like to sit and then settle, while some will more or less drop all

# TROUBLESHOOTING

## The *Settle*

*Rowdy isn't interested in the treat you are using as a lure.*

Find a better treat! Some possibilities are small bits of cheese, beef, chicken, liverwurst, and meat-flavored baby food. Just be sure that the treat is tiny and doesn't violate any dietary restrictions that may be important to your dog's health.

*Rowdy likes the lure but doesn't follow it to the ground.*

Move your hand closer to his nose, and do it more slowly. He may not realize the treat is in your hand if you move too quickly. If he gets grabby, simply close your fist over the treat until he lies down. (If the treat is gooey, try putting it in a small cup or container that you can cover with your hand.)

*Rowdy lowers his head to follow the treat but doesn't lie down.*

Continue to hold the treat near the floor between his front legs, and put your hands between his shoulder blades to model the behavior by gently guiding him down — do not force him down. Mark and give him the treat only when he is all the way down.

*Rowdy lowers his front end, but his fanny stays up in the air.*

Very gently guide his hips downward — but do not force them — to model the *down*. Mark and give him the treat as soon as he's completely down. If he doesn't lower his rear end with light pressure from your hand, don't try to force him down. Instead, keep the hand with the treat close to the ground. With your other arm, cradle your dog's hind legs above the hocks (the point of the joint between the long bones of the upper and lower legs), and gently move your arm forward until he folds down. When he's all the way down, mark and give him the treat.

*Rowdy steps backward instead of lying down.*

Move your hand with the treat a little faster so that he lowers his head more quickly. If that doesn't work, put his leash on and hold it or stand on it so that he can't back up. (Don't pull him forward — just keep him from backing up.)

the way down from the *stand*. You can teach him that "settle" means "lie down, get comfy, and stay there until I release you," or you can give him a separate *stay* command. (See section "Stay.")

## STAY

A dog who will stay in one position and place until released is a credit to his trainer's dedication. He is also often an easier dog to live with, and in some situations, he is safer than he would be otherwise. If you plan to compete with your dog in almost any canine sport or to volunteer your pal as a therapy dog, he absolutely, positively must learn to stay where you tell him. A *sit-*

*stay* is useful for keeping him in place for relatively short stretches of time, like when you open a door before he's allowed to go through it. The *settle-stay* (or *down-stay*) can be useful for longer periods. The *stand-stay* is handy for grooming, vet visits, and some more advanced training situations.

Teaching your dog to stay where you put him is well worth the time and effort, but it is not an easy behavior to teach. Your dog doesn't see any point in staying in one spot (unless he's ready for a snooze), especially if that spot isn't next to you. In fact, having to stay put while you watch from a distance—or even leave the room—can be downright scary for your dog.

Also, teaching a reliable *stay* takes time. How long it will take your dog to learn to stay is purely individual, so don't compare him to his obedience classmates or his litter brother or your second cousin's obedience trial champion. Follow the step-by-step method described here, be patient, and let your dog, not your ego, determine how long the process will take. The biggest mistake people make in trying to teach the *stay* command is rushing the process. If you want your dog to learn to stay, make sure that he is solid at each step before you take the next one, even if it's only a matter of a couple of feet (m) or a few seconds.

*Teaching your dog to stay reliably where you tell him, as this Golden Retriever is doing, will make him a more pleasant dog to have around and can keep him safer in some situations.*

An experienced, skilled obedience instructor often can spot a small training mistake and save you weeks—or years—of frustration by offering a solution based specifically on her observations of you and your dog. By all means, train on your own—practice makes for improvement. But if you're having trouble getting the point across to your furry friend, get thee to some obedience lessons. You'll find that the relatively small investment of money and time will more than pay for itself by making your dog a much more pleasant companion for years to come.

## Before You Start

Before you begin teaching the *stay*, there are two points I'd like to make. First, for some reason, a lot of people seem to think that the louder they make the *stay* command, the more likely their dog is to obey it. In fact, it seems like every time I practice *stays* with a group, there's someone who scares the heck out of the rest of the group with a booming "Stay!" Please don't yell your command. If your dog understands "stay," you can whisper and he will still obey. If he doesn't yet understand, yelling will just increase his stress level, making it more likely that he will "break" (get up from) the *stay*. Second, review the discussion of the release word in Chapter 5. Remember, you must use a formal command to release your dog from the *stay*. If he can move when he chooses to, whether after one minute or ten, you don't really have a successful *stay*.

Be sure to practice *stays* in different situations so that your dog learns that the *stay* means stay no matter where he is or what's going on. The nice thing about *stays* is that, once he has the basics, you can practice while you do other things—watch television, iron, cook. Just don't forget that you told him to stay—if you forget him and he releases himself 10 minutes later, what's to stop him from releasing himself after 30 seconds the next time? If you want your dog to be reliable about following commands, you have to be reliable and consistent about giving them, enforcing them, and releasing him from them.

Although you are positioning your dog in the *settle* position rather than reinforcing his spontaneous behavior, essentially you want to capture the *stay*. (See Chapter 5 for more about capturing.) Some people also model the *settle-stay* (or *down-stay*) by physically pushing the dog into position, but that can easily become a contest of wills and strength if the dog resists. I find it more effective to teach *stay* in very small increments, capturing his successes and rewarding them.

## Teaching *Stay* Step by Step

Depending on your long-term goals, you may want to train your dog to stay on command when he is sitting, lying down, and standing squarely on all four feet. I suggest that you teach *stay* in the *settle* position (lying down and rolled onto one hip) first because it is the easiest position for a dog to hold. When your dog will settle and stay reliably for a minute or so, you can then begin teaching the *sit-stay*, and after that, the *stand-stay*.

### The **Settle-Stay**

Obviously, you first have to teach your dog the *settle* command. (See section "Settle.") As soon as he responds fairly reliably to that command, you can teach him to stay.

1. Start with your dog on leash. Tell him "Settle," luring him down if necessary. When he is in position, tell him "Stay." (You also can teach him a hand signal—the common signal for *stay* is the palm of the hand held briefly in front of the dog's face.)

*Practice short stays initially, and increase your time and distance away from your dog only when he is reliable at the lesser time and distance.*

*Like the settle-stay, the sit-stay is useful when you want your dog to stay put for longer periods.*

2. In the beginning, your dog won't understand "Stay," and he will probably start to get up at some point. When he does, put him back in the *settle* position and tell him "Stay" again. Don't yell or get excited—just calmly reposition your dog and tell him "Stay."

3. If he stays down a few seconds, mark the behavior, reward, and release. Start with very short *stays*—maybe ten seconds—and stand no more than one step from your dog.

4. When he will settle and stay without trying to get up for a solid 10 seconds, you can begin to increase the length of the *stay* by very small increments—10 to 15 seconds—while you remain standing only a step away from your dog. (You can move from his side to stand in front of him at this point if you want to so that he learns that he has to stay no matter where you are.) Work slowly up to a five-minute *settle-stay* with you no more than one step from your dog.

5. When your dog will do the five-minute *stay* reliably, you can start to increase your distance from him. Tell him to settle and stay, then add one step to your distance from him. Be prepared to put him back in position if necessary—he must learn that this is the same exercise as before, even though you are farther away.

6. Ask for a shorter time when you increase distance, and slowly build the time back up. If your dog seems to be comfortable, try increasing the time by 30 seconds on each repetition. If you reach a point when he starts to fidget or get up, shorten your distance and time by half and slowly build the time until he is solid again for five minutes. Then slowly increase your distance again by one or two steps, shortening the time and slowly building it back up to five minutes. The pattern here is increase distance, decrease time, and build back up.

### *The* Sit-Stay

When your dog begins to understand the *settle-stay*, you can teach him the *sit-stay*. Use the same process as you did for the *settle-stay*, except put your dog in a *sit* at the beginning. Even if your dog will do a five-minute *settle-stay* with you in the next county, begin the *sit-stay* at the beginning in terms of time and distance. If he does well, you will be able to increase time and distance more quickly than you did the first time around. But remember, this is a completely new exercise to your dog, so help him get it right.

### *The* Stand-Stay

The *stand-stay* is one of the hardest things for most dogs to learn—after all, how often does anyone just stand completely still? But if you are patient, you can do it!
1. To teach your dog to stand from a *sit*, hold a treat in one hand and place your other hand, palm down, under his belly.
2. Lure him slightly forward with the treat. He will probably stand up. If not, gently touch his belly with the back of your hand

**The Stays in Competition**

In obedience competition, there is an exercise called the "stand for examination" in which a dog must stand and stay without moving his feet while the judge touches him as his handler watches from 6 feet (1.8 m) away. If you plan to compete in obedience, teach your dog to let people touch him while he stays sitting before you attempt a stand for examination. It's much easier for him to move when standing, and if he is wiggly-friendly or shy, you will be constantly correcting him for moving his feet. Wait until he can accept the "sit for examination" calmly before you try it at a stand.

If you plan to compete in obedience, I recommend that you slowly build the time until your dog will stay for at least one minute longer than the time required in competition, which varies from one to five minutes, depending on the level. If you go to the Open level of obedience, your dog will have to stay while you are out of sight, so when he is reliable with you in the same room, begin to leave the room, very briefly at first, then for longer periods. Make sure that you can tell if he moves, though—have a peephole or mirror, or have someone else watch and tell you if he moves.

# TROUBLESHOOTING

## The *Stay*

The biggest mistake that people make in teaching the *stay* is to expect too much too soon. This is a stressful exercise for your dog (and will be for you, too, if you go on to compete in obedience!). Give your dog time to learn not only that he is supposed to stay in one place in one position but also that it's no big deal. You'll be back, he's safe, and you're safe and happy. If you increase your distance from your dog, and/or the length of time you expect him to stay too quickly, you will spend much more time trying to "correct" him for not staying than you will if you simply take your time from the beginning.

*Stay* is a difficult command to follow, no question. Here are some suggestions to prevent or fix the most common problems with this command.

*Rowdy fidgets, squirms, whines, drools, and otherwise appears to be uncomfortable during the stay.*

You have pushed him to the edge of his comfort level, and he will probably break the *stay* soon. To reassure him, move closer to him and reduce the time, then slowly build back up. Be sure to mark the correct behavior and to reward him for staying every so often.

*Rowdy gets up every time you stand 20 feet (6.1 m) away and ask him to stay for three minutes.*

Reduce the distance by half, and slowly increase the time until he does a solid five-minute *stay* while you stand 10 feet (3.0 m) away. Then increase the distance in increments, reducing the time and building it up again with each increase in distance.

*Rowdy was doing solid three-minute stays while you stood 40 feet (12.2 m) away, but now he gets up before the three minutes are up.*

Sometimes training regresses for all sorts of reasons. Whatever the reason, the time and distance you are asking of him now exceed his tolerance. Begin by reducing your distance from him by half. If you were 40 feet away, move 20 feet (6.1 m) closer to your dog. If he is still uncomfortable, cut the distance in half again, to 10 feet (3.0 m). Don't make a big fuss about it, as that will add to his stress level. Just reduce the distance, and when you reach a point where he succeeds, stay there for several sessions and reward him for doing well. Then slowly rebuild your full-length three-minute *stay*.

*Rowdy will sit and stay at home for 10 minutes while you move all around the house, but at obedience class he gets up 30 seconds into the exercise.*

Your dog hasn't generalized the command to different situations, and doggy school is completely different from home—and more stressful. Treat the *stay* at obedience class (and other places) like a new exercise, starting with less time and distance and slowly increasing.

as you lure him forward. Don't push him up, just touch him enough to give him the idea.

3. When he is standing, mark and reward. When he responds reliably to the lure, add the command "Stand," and wean away the lure by using it less and less frequently until you don't need it at all. Continue to mark and reward him for standing, every time at first, then sporadically.

4. To teach your dog to stand from a prone position, follow the same basic sequence, but hold the lure in front of and higher than your dog's head so that he will have to stand up to reach it. At first he may stand and then start to sit, thinking that sitting is the way to get the reward, so have your other hand ready to place gently under his belly as in Step 2.

5. When he stands reliably, add the *stay* command. Follow the procedures for the *settle-stay*, starting with short duration and distance and slowly increasing until you can stand 6 feet (1.8 m) in front of your dog for one minute without him moving at all.

## WALK NICELY ON LEASH

All dogs, regardless of size, age, or lifestyle, should be taught basic leash skills. You should be able to take your dog for a walk around the block or into a crowded veterinary office without having your legs wrapped up or your shoulder dislocated. Even a pint-sized pooch can take the fun out of a walk if he pulls, spins,

*All dogs should learn to walk as politely on leash as this dog is doing.*

# TROUBLESHOOTING

## Walk Nicely on Leash

*Rowdy is such a determined puller that stopping just makes him pull and dance more.*

Move him away from his goal. In other words, when he pulls, rather than simply stopping, turn around and walk the other way. Don't yank your dog, don't talk to him, and don't wait for him. It's his job to pay attention to where you are and to stick with you. Simply hold your leash firmly, turn around, and walk at a normal speed in the other direction. Your dog will have to follow. When he catches up to you, be very happy to see him, and mark and reward him for being with you. Most dogs quickly learn to pay attention and not to pull.

*Rowdy is a dedicated puller who won't respond to any of your training tactics.*

He may need a different collar or a head halter for a while to give you better control. Of course, it may also be that you are inadvertently encouraging him to pull by hurrying along with him. In either case, your best option is to take an obedience class or even a few private lessons from a qualified instructor who can help you get your dog under control.

*Rowdy weaves back and forth or runs circles around you.*

Lure him into position beside you with a treat. When he takes a few steps in the right place, mark that behavior with your voice or clicker, and reward him. Repeat until he stays beside you, slowly increasing the time between treats until he no longer needs to be lured and rewarded. If his weaving or circling is wild enough to pose a risk, shorten your leash so that he has to stay on one side of you, and reward him when he does.

and jerks you around, and good leash skills are also important for safety, both your dog's and your own. When he is properly leash trained, your dog will walk steadily on one side of you with the leash slack. Like many other aspects of good training, teaching him to do this will require some time and effort, but the payoff is a dog who is a pleasure to walk.

## Before You Start

Begin by checking your equipment. Your dog needs an appropriate collar that fits him properly, as well as a suitable leash. (See Chapter 4.) In the beginning, you should have treats or some other reward for your dog and your clicker if you use one to mark good behavior.

If you have a puppy or an adult who has never been leash

trained, begin with short, positive sessions. For most sports, dogs are taught to walk on the handler's left side, but if you don't plan to compete and prefer to have your dog on your right, that's your choice. It is a good idea, though, to teach your dog to stay on one side so that he doesn't trip you as he runs back and forth.

To stop your dog from pulling, you can capture his nonpulling behavior. To teach him to walk beside you, a combination of capturing, luring, and modeling usually works well.

## Teaching *Walk Nicely on Leash* Step by Step

### *Walking Without Pulling*

1. Begin by capturing your dog's correct behavior on leash. Even if he's a whirling dervish or major-league puller, there will be

*A dog who pulls on leash poses a danger to himself and the person walking him.*

times when he stops the craziness enough to let the leash go slack. He may even turn to look at you (probably to find out why you're plodding along).

2. The instant the leash goes slack, mark and reward.

3. If your dog walks pretty nicely without pulling or dancing, mark and reward him every so often to give him a "reference point." If he understands that you like him to walk calmly without pulling and he gets excited and forgets his manners somewhere down the road, be sure to mark and reward him when he resumes polite walking.

If your dog has already formed the habit of pulling on his leash, you must convince him of two things: Pulling will not hasten his arrival at his goal, and walking politely will make you happy enough

*If you keep your dog's leash reasonably short, he won't be able to leave your side as easily.*

to reward him. If you are training a puppy, or if your adult dog is responsive and submissive to you, try the "no forward progress" approach to pulling. In other words, teach your dog that if he tries to pull you toward something, you will stop in your tracks. If your dog is determined to get where he wants to go, he may not notice right away that you are playing statue, but sooner or later he will either stop pulling or turn and look at you. The instant the leash goes slack, mark and reward, and then resume walking. If your dog pulls again, stop again. You may have to spend a few days going for short, slow walks, but many dogs figure out very quickly that pulling slows progress rather than speeds it up.

### *Walking by Your Side*

Your dog also needs to learn to stay on one side of you. (The left side is traditional.) If he constantly weaves back and forth or runs around you in circles, your walk won't be much fun, and you could trip and injure yourself or your dog. If your dog tends to wander back and forth or circle you, you can use a combination of luring and modeling techniques to show him what you want:

1. Keep your dog's leash short enough that he cannot easily leave your side, thereby modeling the position you want him to be in. Don't keep it so short that you're dragging him, though.
2. Simultaneously lure him into the correct area by your side with tiny treats. You can mark the behavior with a word or clicker if you like.
3. When he starts to get the idea, stop luring, but do reward him for staying by your side. Give a treat every few steps at first, increasing the distance you walk between treats until he forms the habit of walking at your side without treats. You also can give him a bit more leash as long as he doesn't weave or circle.

If you train your dog only to do the things covered in this chapter—come when called, sit, settle, stay, and walk politely on leash—you will have a dog who is more secure, easier to live with, and no doubt the envy of most of your friends and family. Of course, as important as they are, these commands are just the beginning, and you may find that you enjoy the training process as much as the results. If so, keep reading—in the next chapter, we'll explore more advanced training possibilities.

# ADVANCED TRAINING

In the last chapter, we discussed five basic commands that will go a long way toward making your dog a better, more confident companion. But why stop there? Your dog is certainly capable of learning much more, and you are capable of teaching him. So in this chapter, I suggest six more excellent skills to teach your dog. They will make life more interesting for him and easier for you. In addition, some of them are stepping stones to even more advanced training, and some—especially *leave it*, *give*, and *wait*—are important for your dog's safety. So grab your gear and let's do some more training.

## DOWN

Many people use the *down* as an all-purpose "lie down on the ground" command, but I teach *down* separately from *settle*. (See Chapter 7.) The terms don't matter—you could, for instance, use the word "down" in place of my "settle," and "drop" in place of my "down." It's the distinction between the two types of "flat on the floor" behaviors that is important. The *settle*, as we learned, indicates a position in which the dog lies rolled onto one hip, with one leg tucked under him, his belly and feet more or less on one side, his spine tilted toward the floor on the other side. This is a relaxed posture that your dog can stay in for an extended period of time, and he has to "work" a little to get up from a settle. *Down*, in contrast, indicates a "sphinx" position in which the dog lies balanced on his chest and belly without rolling in either direction. His elbows and all four feet are under him, pads toward the ground. This is a less relaxed posture, so it's not very comfortable for long *stays*, but your dog can drop into this position and rise out of it very quickly, even when moving at a fast pace, which is why the command is considered a more advanced form of training than the simple *settle* command described in Chapter 7.

There are times when a quick *down* (and *stay* in that position) is the safest thing for your dog—safer even than calling him to you. Everyone has occasionally had a dog get away—someone leaves a gate open, a leash breaks, a door opens at the wrong moment. If your dog is across the street and a car is coming, you can't call him to you without putting him at risk, but if he will lie down quickly on command and stay down until you release him, you have control and a safe dog. Oddly enough, the *down* is also sometimes more effective than the

*The* down *command should be part of every dog's basic education, as this German Shepherd puppy is learning.*

*recall* if your dog is loose and playing "you can't catch me." If you decide to train your dog for obedience competition (see Chapter 10) beyond the Novice level, you will have to teach a "moving *down*" in which he lies down from a trot in the Open class and a "signal *down*" in which he lies down from a standing position in the Utility class. You can incorporate the beginning of a hand signal into your dog's early training so that eventually he will respond to both the verbal command and the signal.

## Prerequisites and Equipment

Your dog doesn't need to know any other commands to learn *down*, but he should be familiar with your marker. He needs to understand that your marker, whether the click of a clicker or a word, means "Good job, a reward is coming." (See Chapter 5, "Markers.")You may want to put your dog on leash to keep him with you until he's ready for "distance *downs*," and you will need your marker and treats.

I want my dog's response to the *down* command to be almost a reflex, so I prefer to teach it from a *stand*, not from a *sit*. Skipping the intermediary *sit* eliminates one command and gets your dog into the *down* position more quickly.

You can capture and shape the *down* commands, but to speed things up, I suggest luring and modeling training techniques.

## Teaching "*Down*" Step by Step

### The Down *From a Stand*

1. Begin by luring your dog from the *stand* position into the *down* position. (If he's a puppy or a small dog, you may want to kneel when you begin this training.) Start with your dog standing. Hold a treat in your hand, let your dog know it's there, and slowly move your hand under his chin toward and then between his front legs, lowering it toward the floor as you go.

2. As his head follows the treat, his shoulders will fold downward, and hopefully his rear end will follow suit. If he lowers his head or head and shoulders without lowering his rear end, you can gently guide him into the *down* position by applying light pressure to his shoulders and/or hips, thus modeling the behavior you want.

3. As soon as his elbows and rear are all the way down, mark and reward him with the treat. At that point, you can either release him before you repeat the procedure, or you can teach the stand command (see Chapter 7) so that he learns to contrast "down" and "stand."

4. As your dog responds more quickly to the lure and command, you can begin to wean him from the lure by gradually reducing the distance your hand travels toward the floor until you don't have to lure him at all. When he is dropping to the *down* position reliably on command without the lure, continue to mark his correct behavior, but reward him with a treat less and less frequently. You also can begin to mark and reward only faster and faster responses, and only when he stays in the *down* position for longer and longer periods before you mark, reward, and release him.

### The Down *While Moving*

When your dog understands what "down" means when standing still, you can begin to teach him to down while moving. In fact, many dogs enjoy this game and are actually better at going down while moving than from a *stand*.

**Sex and Aggression**

Sexually intact (unneutered) animals are much more likely to fight or bite than their altered counterparts. Although most intact dogs are every bit as trainable as their altered brethren, in some cases, higher levels of sex hormones can make the dog aggressive enough to resist training that puts them in submissive positions. You can greatly reduce conflict among your dogs and reduce the risk that your dog will bite someone by having him or her altered (spayed or neutered).

# TROUBLESHOOTING

## The *Down*

If you have trouble teaching your dog to down, use the troubleshooting methods for the *settle* (see Chapter 7), but start from a *stand* and do not roll your dog onto his hip.

If you are taking your dog to obedience classes, and he refuses to drop to the *down* position in that environment, he may be reluctant to assume a submissive position around strange dogs. This is often especially true of small dogs, who may be nervous around their larger brethren. In this case, work hard on the *down* command at home until your dog really understands it. Then take him to different places — parks, school parking lots, and so forth — and practice there. Begin in places with low levels of activity, and slowly move to environments with more activity.

1. Begin by walking with your dog beside you and with a treat in your hand.
2. Stop and simultaneously lure him into the down with the treat.
3. When he's all the way down, mark and reward, then say "Let's go" and continue walking with him.
4. Do a few of these "random *downs*," and then quit.

When your dog will drop reliably beside you, start dropping him at other times, and use rewards other than treats to reinforce his correct responses. For instance, if your dog loves to play ball, have him drop to the *down* position before you throw the ball. Rather than always having him sit for his dinner, vary what he has to do—like settle or down.

Variety, as they say, is the spice of life, and that's just as true for your dog as for you. The more you vary the situations in which your dog is required to respond to a command, the more reliable he will become, because he will understand the command itself, not just a specific context in which you give it.

## TOUCH THE TARGET

Targeting—in which your dog learns to touch a designated object with his nose or paws—is a fun exercise on its own and is also useful for teaching your dog many things. Targets are commonly used for trick training and in obedience, agility, and

*Targeting teaches a dog to touch a designated object with his nose or paws.*

other types of advanced training. They are useful, too, for teaching some household behaviors, such as *go to bed*. (See section "Go to Bed.")

## Prerequisites and Equipment

As with the *down*, your dog must understand that your marker, whether the click of a clicker or a word, means "good job, a reward is coming." (See Chapter 5, "Markers.") You need a target, which can be almost anything your dog can see. Many trainers use their own palm or fingers as a target for some kinds of training. Plastic lids are good targets—they're cheap, easy to find, and fit into pockets, and they come in different sizes. Just be sure to clean any food off the lid before your dog does! A "target stick" is good for teaching movements, such as heeling or a spin. Commercial target sticks are available, or you can use a dowel rod or the adjustment rod from a venetian blind with a strip of colored tape wrapped around one end. You can even use a piece of tape stuck to a wall or fence. Once your dog learns to touch one target, you can easily transfer his targeting to other objects as needed. If you are not in a secure area, or if your dog has a tendency to wander away during training, put a leash on him.

We will teach targeting by capturing your dog's behavior when he spontaneously goes to the target and by luring him when he doesn't.

### Teaching Your Dog to Touch a Target Step by Step

1. Select your target—I will use a small plastic lid for my example.
2. Hold the lid where your dog can reach it, or toss it on the floor.
3. When he goes to it, mark and treat. Don't tell him to do anything yet; just let him figure out that every time he touches the target with his nose, you mark and give him a treat.
4. If he doesn't return to the target after the first sniff or touch, move it to get his interest. If necessary, put a treat on the target, and the instant your dog touches the target to take the treat,

# TROUBLESHOOTING
## Touch the Target

*Rowdy bites or licks the target.*

You are probably waiting too long to mark. Be sure to mark the instant his nose touches the target—he should then turn to you for the treat that follows the marker. Unless, of course, there's food on that target lid! If necessary, you can mark several times just before he touches the target to prevent the bite or lick, then go back to marking the nose touch.

*Rowdy looks at the target but doesn't touch it.*

Mark his behavior when he gets close to the target, and reward him. Gradually wait until he's closer and closer before you mark and reward. Eventually he will get close enough to touch the target.

*Rowdy shows no interest in the target.*

Try to make the target more interesting. Put a really yummy treat on top of the target, and the instant your dog touches it, mark his behavior (which is self-rewarding because the treat is already there). When he has touched it and gotten his treat a few times, place a treat under the target, and mark his behavior when he touches the target as he looks for the treat. If he doesn't get the treat himself, move the target and let him have the reward. After he has touched the target with the treat under it a few times, put the target down without the treat, then mark his behavior when he touches the target and reward him—make the reward extra special the first few times.

*Take a break from training to play with your dog.*

mark his behavior. When he has done that a few times, put the target down without the food. When he investigates, mark and give him a treat.

5. Repeat the touch or sniff | mark | reward sequence five or six times, then quit and do something else for a while. Be sure to remove the target.

6. When your dog is reliably touching the target with his nose, add your cue—"touch," "go touch," or "target" are commonly used. You also can make the targeting more challenging—hold the target in your hand and move it so that your dog has to follow it to touch it. Put it in different places.

Some dogs are able to grasp this concept almost immediately, while others need a few short sessions to figure out that touching the target makes you mark and treat.

Eventually, the target itself will become rewarding for your dog because he associates it with good things—your mark and treat. Many trainers use their own hands as "target" rewards in competition, teaching their dogs to jump and touch to relieve stress and reinforce good performances.

## GO TO BED

As much as you love your dog, there are times when he really needs to get out of the way. You can, of course, lock him in his crate or in another room or put him out in the backyard, but it's much nicer for everyone if you can just tell him to go to a special place and stay there. You can use any command you like for this—I like "Go to bed."

### Prerequisites and Equipment

To teach *go to bed*, first teach your dog to touch a target (see section "Touch the Target") and to settle and stay. (See Chapter 7.) You will need a target, something to indicate the place where your dog will lie (a dog bed or rug works well since he's going to lie down and stay there for a while), a marker, and a reward.

The methods you use will depend on how quickly your dog is able to combine the *touch the target*, *settle*, and *stay* commands he has already learned but may include capturing, luring, and possibly modeling the behavior you want.

### Teaching *Go to Bed* Step by Step

Although this may seem like a pretty straightforward command to us, it requires your dog to combine three different maneuvers

# TROUBLESHOOTING

## Go to Bed

*Rowdy doesn't seem to understand what you want him to do.*

Go back to basic targeting until he will go to and touch a target across the room from you.

*Rowdy goes to his bed but doesn't settle and stay there.*

Go back to basic training until he will quickly settle, relax, and stay for at least five minutes when you tell him to.

*Rowdy goes to his place, settles, and stays for a short time, then gets up and comes to you.*

Review the procedure for teaching the *stay* command. Consider moving Rowdy's bed closer to where you will be for initial go-to-bed training, and then increase the distance from you in small increments until his spot is back where you want it and he is comfortable staying that distance from you.

## When Will Your Dog Be an Adult?

Dogs develop at different rates, but in general, small dogs mature sooner than big dogs. Some toy breeds are fully grown by seven or eight months. Many medium and large dogs don't finish gaining height until they are 12 to 18 months old and may not be really mature for another year or two. It's hard sometimes to remember that a 60-pound (27.2-kg) dynamo is still a puppy, but it's important to realize that no matter how big your dog's body has grown, he is still a puppy mentally and emotionally for the first two to three years of his life. Although you can begin teaching him more advanced commands, it's not fair to expect an immature dog to perform reliably.

into what we perceive as one response. He must go to a specific place, settle there, and stay. So to help him get the idea, we'll break the parts down for him.

1. Begin by taking your dog to his place. If he will follow you there without a leash, that's fine, but use a leash if you need to.
2. Tell him "Settle" and "Stay," and work on building up the length of time he will stay there before being released. Eventually, you should be able to send him to his place and he should stay there for a fairly long time (30 minutes or longer) without getting up. When he will settle and stay for a reasonable length of time (I'd suggest ten minutes minimum), it's time to teach him to go to his place on his own.
3. Show your dog the target and have him touch it once or twice to warm up.
4. Put him in a *sit-stay* a few feet (m) from his place, put the target on his place, and return to your dog. Tell him "Touch," and when he gets to the target and touches it, tell him "Settle."
5. If he tends to want to return to you after touching the target, stand closer to his place or step toward it while he's moving toward the target.
6. When he will touch the

*Go to bed teaches your dog to go to his place and stay there.*

At 16 months of age as I write this, my Labrador Retriever puppy, Lily, still snitches things from my study—socks are a favorite. Ever since she was a tiny puppy, I have always shown her how pleased I am when she brings me things: "Oh, Lily, what do you have? How wonderful!" As a result, she brings these treasures to me, eyes smiling and tail wagging, and happily hands them over in exchange for a butt scratch and praise. Finding and carrying things is pleasurable for dogs. Make giving them back equally pleasurable, and you'll both be much happier.

target and settle quickly and reliably, begin to say "Go to bed, touch," and when he gets there, "Settle."

7. When he goes reliably, stop saying "Touch," but continue to reward him for going to his place. Then progress to rewarding him only after he settles. When he is responding immediately as soon as (or even before) you say "Settle," eliminate that command but don't reward him until he lies down.

8. Now when you tell your dog "Go to bed," he should go there, settle, and stay. Be sure to mark that behavior even if you don't give him a reward.

## GIVE

The *give* command teaches your dog to "hand it over." Although many people never teach their dogs to give things when told, there are several reasons to teach this important command. Obviously, being able to take things away from your dog could save his life. It also could save your other possessions from being mangled or eaten. You'll be able to play fetch with your dog without having to wrestle the ball away from him. Teaching your dog to give things up to you, whether for a few seconds or for good, also reinforces your superior position in the household pack.

For safety, exercise some caution when teaching *give*. Some dogs who willingly give up toys and sticks and shoes are more defensive about food, so do not use food to teach this command until your dog obeys it reliably with other things. If your dog tends to guard

*The* give *command teaches a dog to relinquish what he has in his possession.*

# TROUBLESHOOTING

## The *Give*

**Rowdy plays keep-away, showing you things but not giving them to you.**

Take a two-pronged approach. **1.** Don't ever chase him or grab at him when he teases you with something. If it's something that he really shouldn't have, get something else that's really good (in his eyes) to trade for it. When he drops what he has, give him the good stuff and quietly take the "treasure" away. (Don't offer an alternate and then withhold it as "punishment"—your dog will catch on very quickly to that ploy, and it will be harder than ever to take anything from him.) **2.** Set up training sessions to teach *give* rather than waiting for spontaneous offers. Put a leash on your dog and give him a toy, then use the training guidelines, trading him for the toy and then giving it back to him. Repeat several times, then give him the toy and take the leash off and ignore him unless he brings you the toy on his own. If he does, take it and give him some extra treats. Make a big fuss the first few times he does this so that he learns that giving you things is much more fun than playing keep-away.

**Rowdy still won't trade his item for the treat in your hand.**

You need to take the item from him. Don't play tug-of-war, though—you don't want to teach him to fight you for things. Instead, gently place one hand over the top of his muzzle with your fingers on his upper lips on one side, your thumb on the other. Hold the item with your other hand, but don't pull on it. Very gently press his lips into his teeth and tell him "Give." Increase the pressure against his teeth until he releases his grip, then mark the release, take the toy, let go of his muzzle, give him a treat, and make a big fuss about what a good dog he is. (Also, see warning on page 167.) If your dog is not already on leash, put his leash on, offer the toy, and repeat the "Give" several times. Offer to trade with him, but if he doesn't accept your offer, use the muzzle grip to take the toy.

food or other things by growling, snapping, or biting (see Chapter 9), get professional help to stop the guarding. And teach children never to take things away from a dog, even a dog they know, and especially a dog who tends to guard resources.

## Prerequisites and Equipment

The most important prerequisite for teaching the *give* command is your confidence in your dog's nonaggressive temperament and his respect for you. If you have any concern that your dog may bite you if you take things from him, get help from a qualified canine behaviorist. If you are sure of your dog and are ready to proceed, you will need a collar and leash and toys and/or treats to reward him initially for giving you things.

This method of teaching *give* uses capturing and luring.

## Teaching *Give* Step by Step

If you want your dog to give you things, take a tip from the

*The* give *command teaches your dog to relinquish something he shouldn't have in his possession.*

people who train hunting dogs to retrieve—always be happy when your dog brings you anything, even if it's that disgusting glob he found by the back fence or one of your brand-new designer shoes. The idea is to make your dog want to give you things. If you grumble and growl when you take things from him, why should he want to give you anything?

### Training the Willing Giver

If your dog brings things to you and willingly lets you take them, you're way ahead of the game.

1. Use his spontaneous offers of toys and sticks to reinforce the positive value of giving so that when he has something you really need to take from him, he will already know that giving you things is a good thing to do.

2. If he shows you the toy he has in his mouth, ooh and aah and take it, look at it, and then give it back or toss it. Teach him that you don't always keep the things he gives you.

### Training the Unwilling Giver

1. If your dog brings you things but plays a "look but don't take" game, begin to teach *give* by trading him for what he has. If he's very toy driven, he might trade you one toy for another. Or you can trade a treat for his "treasure."

2. Let him see that you have something for him, and then if possible, take hold of the toy in his mouth. Don't pull on it, just hold it. Offer the treat.

3. When he lets go of the toy to take the treat, mark and reward.

4. When he gets the idea, tell him "Give" when you grasp the toy.

5. When he reliably lets go, begin to wean away the treats, giving them only sporadically and rewarding him instead by giving back the toy or tossing it, or by scratching his ear or butt. The idea behind the treats is to motivate him in the beginning to release the toy, not to "buy" it from him every time.

6. Continue to reinforce the idea that giving you things is good for him—that way, when you really need to take something dangerous or valuable, you will be less likely to meet resistance.

**Warning:** I teach my dogs that I have the right to take anything from them, and I've been known to fish food (and more of those disgusting blobs than I care to think about) right out of their mouths. But *be careful*. If your dog growls when you try to take things from him, get professional help. (See Chapter 9, "Resource Guarding.") Children should not attempt to take things from your dog unless he gives them up spontaneously.

**Always Praise for Obedience**

Once your dog understands *give* and *leave it*, you won't need treats or trade-offs to reinforce him for leaving or giving things, but do remember to praise him for obeying these commands. We all know how hard is to resist temptation or to give up things we like.

## LEAVE IT

The *leave it* command teaches your dog not to touch something. This command will let you tell your dog not to touch the dog next to him at obedience class, your pizza sitting on the coffee table (although I wouldn't leave the room!), and that revolting pile of who-knows-what lying just off the sidewalk.

As with give, exercise caution when teaching *leave it*, and again, do not use food to teach this command until your dog obeys it reliably with other things.

### Prerequisites and Equipment

To teach *leave it* successfully, you need two things: a reward that is worthwhile to your dog and control of the situation so that he doesn't reward himself for ignoring you by getting whatever he's after. Use a really special treat for the reward, and put your dog on leash so that you can control where he goes.

We teach this by preventing the dog from getting to the thing you want him to leave alone and by rewarding him for complying.

### Teaching *Leave It* Step by Step

1. Begin with a "setup" (or take advantage of training opportunities that pop up on walks). Put something that you

# TROUBLESHOOTING

## The *Leave It*

**Rowdy gets the object he's after before you are able to get him away from it.**

You need to get the object back. If it's a toy, use your *give* command to take it away from him, put it back where it was, and repeat the training routine—and make sure that he doesn't get it again! If it's food, take it from him if you can do so safely. If not, start over and adjust your timing and the length of your leash. Put the food in a ventilated container so that your dog can smell it but cannot eat it.

**Rowdy won't give you the object he has.**

Go back to training *give*. If your dog guards the object aggressively, be careful and get professional help.

know your dog will find interesting on the floor or a low table. It can be just about anything that he is likely to try to investigate or pick up, but don't use anything that he is normally allowed to have. (That just wouldn't be fair.)

2. Have your wonderful treats in your pocket or training pouch.

3. Put the leash on your dog. Walk your dog near the set-up item, making sure that the leash is short enough to prevent him from getting it.

4. When he begins to show interest in the set-up object, say "Leave it!" and walk quickly away—he'll have to follow you because of the leash.

5. As soon as your dog looks at you instead of the set-up object mark that behavior and reward him. Make a big, happy fuss about what a good dog he is.

6. Repeat the process three or four times, then quit for this session. When you practice the next time, use a different set-up object. Most dogs begin to respond within a few sessions.

## WAIT

I like to teach my dogs a *wait* command in addition to the *stay*. (See Chapter 7.) The main distinction between *stay* and *wait*, aside from the command itself, is that at the end of a *stay* your dog is simply released—he's "off duty" until you decide to have him do something else. *Wait*, on the other hand, is more like "get set"—your dog needs to hold the position he's in while he waits for further instructions. It is frequently used to set a dog up for a *recall*.

## Prerequisites and Equipment

*Sit*, *down*, or *settle* is useful for teaching *wait* but not absolutely required. Your dog can learn to wait while standing, too. You will probably want to use a leash until he will wait reliably, and you need your marker and treats.

## Teaching *Wait* Step by Step

To teach your dog to wait, follow the directions for teaching *stay* (see Chapter 7), but tell him "Wait" instead of "Stay," and rather than releasing your dog, give him another command after he waits.

*The wait command is similar to the stay but alerts your dog that another command is coming soon. This dog is ready for whatever comes next.*

### Wait *at Doors and Gates*

I just hate having a dog jump around, push, and shove while waiting for a door to open, and then shove his way out as soon as he can squeeze through. Such behavior is not only annoying, it's potentially hazardous for the dog and for whoever is opening the door or standing outside. There's no reason your dog can't wait politely at an open door until you tell him he can go through it.

1. To teach your dog to wait before going through a door or gate, begin with his leash on. Be consistent—don't ever let him charge through a door. (If he does manage to get past you, go get him, put his leash on if it isn't already, bring him back inside, close the door, and start again.)

2. If you are letting your dog out the back door into your fenced yard, tell him to sit and wait before you open the door. Hold the leash fairly short, but don't pull it tight.

3. Open the door by stages. If your dog breaks the *wait* command as you reach for the handle, withdraw your hand, put him back in a *sit,* and tell him "Wait."

4. When he can wait until you grip the door handle, progress to turning the handle, pulling the door open a little and eventually pulling it open all the way. At each stage, withdraw if your dog doesn't wait politely.

5. When he will wait politely until the door is fully open, remove his leash, having him wait until it is completely off.

6. When you (not your dog!) are ready, give him a command to signal the end of his wait. I like the word "exit" because it doesn't conflict with the *go out* command in obedience (which means "go to the other end of the ring"), but use whatever works for you.

7. When your dog will wait reliably with his leash on, you can take the next step, having him wait without a leash while you open the door. Hold his collar lightly if you must, until he is very steady with a door wide open.

## Wait *Out the Door*

If you are exiting through a door with your dog on leash, the risk of being bruised, toppled, or dragged down the steps is even greater than if you're letting him out by himself. He should not pull you out the door but should wait politely until you give permission for him to walk through the opening. Follow the same procedures as for waiting at doors and gates, except use "Let's go" as you step

# TROUBLESHOOTING
## The *Wait*

*Rowdy has trouble learning to wait for a recall—that is, to sit, wait without moving while you walk away and turn to face him, and then come when called.*

We tend to see the whole exercise as one thing, but to your dog, it's a series of discreet units—a *sit*, a *wait*, and a *recall*. Training problems usually arise when the dog is rushed through one or more of the steps.

If your dog tends to get up before you call him, stop calling him from the *wait*. Teach the *wait* and the *recall* separately until your dog knows both of them really well. Teach the *wait* and add distance as you did the stay, and never call your dog from a *wait* until he will wait without moving for a full minute. Go back to him and reward him occasionally, then leave again. Practice the *recall* by having someone hold your dog while you walk away and then call him. Don't say "Wait" or "Stay," just go. He needs to learn to wait on his own, without anyone holding him, so shorten your distance and time and build up slowly if necessary, as you did for with the *stay*. When he is completely solid on the *wait* and does a nice, quick *recall*, you can begin to put the two together, telling him to wait while you walk away, then calling him to you.

*Rowdy still has trouble with the* wait.

You may be increasing the increments too quickly. Be patient. Let your dog figure out that if he gets pushy, the door won't open and you won't reach for it. Don't forget to mark proper, polite behavior and to reward your dog when he gets it right.

*The* wait *command will keep your dog from charging out of the crate.*

through the door together, and keep his leash on if it's walk time.

## Wait *at the Crate*

A dog who charges out of his crate is a nuisance and can endanger himself and whoever opens the crate.

1. To teach your dog not to charge out of his crate, you can follow the same procedure as in "Wait at Doors and Gates" except that you will use the crate door instead of his leash to enforce the *wait*.
2. If he jumps around and pushes on the door when you reach for the latch, withdraw your hand until he's quiet. Try again. Every time he gets silly, withdraw your hand.
3. Proceed to opening the latch, then open the door a tiny fraction at a time.

4. When he waits nicely, mark that behavior and slip him a treat. If he tries to push his way out, close the door.
5. Your dog should wait in his crate until you tell him to come out. (Find a word to tell him that.) Not only will he not clobber you, but you'll be able to hold him there until you put his leash on if necessary.

**Note:** For safety reasons, make sure that your dog is not wearing his leash or training collar when he's in his crate.

Training can be frustrating—trust me, I know that very well! Then again, look how far you've both come. Sure, your dog still makes mistakes, and you still say the wrong thing or tangle your leash up with your treat from time to time. But if you have taught everything I've covered so far, your dog now knows or is learning 11 commands. Put this book down for five minutes, gaze into your dog's eyes, and spend a moment appreciating your dog, yourself, and above all, the strength of the bond that the two of you are forging. Then come back—there's always more to learn!

### The Formal Obedience Recall

Training for obedience competition is beyond the scope of this book, so I don't deal with the formal *recall* with a *front* and *finish*. But for what it's worth, if you plan to compete, I strongly suggest that you teach the *front* and the *finish*, which follow the *recall*, as separate pieces and put the entire sequence— wait|come|front|finish— together only when your dog performs each one reliably by itself.

*Chapter*

# MANAGING UNWANTED BEHAVIORS

ogs, like people, form behavioral habits. According to some studies, it may take as few as three repetitions of a behavior for a habit to form. Some doggy habits are good—pooping in the back corner of the yard, chewing a chew toy while you read the paper, reminding you that it's time for walkies. Other habits are not so good, at least by human definition. And bad habits, as we all know, are hard to change. In the long run, it's much easier to prevent unwanted behaviors than to fix them. You can do this by following seven major steps to help your dog behave himself:

1. **Anticipate what your dog might do.** Canine behaviors are pretty predictable, so you should be able to anticipate many potential problems. Puppies chew things. Untrained dogs don't know not to potty in the house. Dogs dig and bark and eat things. You know all this, so why not plan ahead and prevent your dog from doing things he shouldn't? If you can prevent your dog from forming a bad habit, all the better. If you can keep him from indulging in a bad habit for long enough and replace it with a good one, he'll stop doing it.

2. **Provide an alternative behavior** to replace the one you don't like whenever possible. It's much easier to teach your dog to do something than to teach him to do nothing.

3. **Evaluate why your dog is behaving as he is.** Is he responding to an instinct to dig or chase things? Is he going through a developmental stage such as teething? Is he bored and full of energy? Has he trained you? ("If I stare at the human and bark, she'll get up and give me a biscuit!") Is he frightened? Is he ill or in pain? Have you inadvertently taught him that it's okay to do what he's doing?

4. **Exercise your dog.** A tired dog is a good dog. How much exercise your dog needs will depend in part on his breed or mixture of breeds. (See Chapter 2.) If he was designed to be a lap warmer, 20 minute of chasing a ball in the living room may be all he needs. If his forebears rounded up and guarded livestock, he probably needs at least an hour of running exercise every day. His age and physical health also will affect how much exercise he needs. In any case, it's up to you to get your dog moving. Most won't self-exercise, so sending your dog to the backyard alone doesn't count.

5. **Stimulate your dog's mind.** Dogs are intelligent animals, and intelligence demands to be used. If you don't provide mental stimulation, your dog will probably find his own, and chances are you won't like what he finds. Physical exercise provides some mental stimulation—your dog sees new things when you go for walks and solves problems when his ball rolls under the couch or into a shrub. You also can play games with him—hide a toy and have him find it, or teach him some tricks. You can find dog toys that are designed as puzzles—the dog has to figure out how to get a treat out of the toy. Formal training in obedience, agility, tracking, and breed-specific activities also provide mental and physical exercise.

6. **Train your dog.** I don't mean just in the problem area, although that will help. But a dog who learns to behave and obey in one setting usually behaves better in other settings. That may be partly because he expends physical and mental energy when training, but it's also because training helps him understand and trust you, and that makes him more secure and less likely to engage in problem behaviors. If you do run into a problem behavior you can't control or that is dangerous, ask your vet to refer you to a qualified professional dog trainer or behaviorist. Don't let a small problem become a big one.

7. **Take charge.** You (and all the human members of your household) need to rank higher than your dog in the "pack" hierarchy. (See Chapter 2.) If your dog is pushy, turn the tables on him. Make him earn what he wants by responding to a command. Teach him some tricks (see Chapter 10) so that you don't both get bored with *sit* and *down*. Then have him dance for his dinner, bow to go outdoors, or roll over for a walk. If he's in your way, make him move rather than going around him. If he's sleeping in your favorite chair, make him get off if you want to sit down. He will not see your behavior as rude or unfair—he will see it as the normal behavior of a higher-ranking individual. You'll both be happier if your dog knows that you are in charge.

*Try to anticipate what your dog might do when faced with temptation, and be proactive about preventing the problem. This Golden Retriever's "counter surfing" could be prevented by removing temptation when he's unsupervised.*

*One of the best ways to prevent unwanted behavior is to be sure that your dog gets plenty of exercise every day.*

If your dog already has an unwanted behavior, rest assured—there are many ways to correct it. However, I do not recommend punishment. Dogs should not be spanked, yanked, or otherwise roughed up physically or mentally. Those methods are not only cruel, but they are ineffective in the long run. Yes, you may be able to bully your dog out of a behavior, but at the same time, you will teach him to mistrust you. Unfortunately, some very nice, generally kind people advocate or use abusive methods of managing dogs without meaning to. So before you act or react, think about what you are doing and review Chapter 5, as well as the pertinent parts of Chapters 6, 7, and 8.

The following are some common doggy problem behaviors and some training solutions to help you manage them.

## AGGRESSION

Some dogs have unstable or aggressive temperaments. Pain or illness can cause behavioral changes, including aggression. Fear also can cause a dog to bite. An aggressive dog—one who threatens to bite, tries to bite, or does bite in inappropriate circumstances—is

Dogs don't bluff, and they almost never bite without giving fair warning, sometimes over the course of several encounters. If your dog's hair stands on end (especially along his spine), if he stands with stiff legs and his tail straight up, or if he growls and bares his teeth, he is being as clear as he can be. Unfortunately, people — especially children — don't always get the message. Some people even think threatening behavior is funny, especially in small dogs. But dog bites are no joke, and even one bite could result in a serious injury. It could also result in the death of your dog and an expensive lawsuit. So if your dog bites or threatens to bite you or anyone else, get professional help immediately.

dangerous. (The only appropriate circumstance is a real threat as defined in human terms—for instance, an attacker or burglar in your home.) Dog bites are not funny, and even a small dog can cause serious damage and pain.

## Management Techniques

If your dog behaves aggressively toward people or other animals, you need to get qualified professional help immediately.

### *Take Your Dog to the Veterinarian*

Begin by taking your dog to your veterinarian for a thorough physical, and be sure that she knows about the aggression problem. Ask for a full thyroid panel (not just a thyroid screening), as low thyroid sometimes causes aggressive behavior and cannot always be diagnosed from the simple screening. Ask your vet's advice about other testing—some diseases can cause aggression. Sexually intact dogs (not neutered) are more likely to behave aggressively, so if your dog is intact, have him neutered or her spayed. Altering is more effective if done before the animal reaches sexual maturity but may help to reduce aggression in some adult dogs too.

*A tired puppy is a good puppy, especially when he's asleep like this Toy Poodle!*

### Contact a Behaviorist

Behavioral approaches are also effective in reducing aggression in some dogs, but be careful in your selection of a behaviorist. Some are well qualified to deal with aggression, but many are not. Ask your vet or obedience instructor for referrals, and then check the person's credentials. What training has she had as a general canine behaviorist and as a specialist in aggression? What methods does she use? The last thing you want is an abusive trainer—but you do need someone who is able to manage your dog safely. Ask for references to other clients she has worked with, and talk to them—find out whether the treatment was successful. Keep in mind that some dogs simply cannot be made into safe pets, and a good behaviorist will be honest about that fact. Beware of anyone who claims to be able to fix any problem. Find out exactly what the evaluation and training will involve, what it will cost, and what the odds are that your dog will become safe and reliable in your home environment. Also, ask how you and your family will be included in the process—it will do you no good if the behaviorist can manage your dog but you can't.

### Make Safety a Priority

Regardless of its cause, safety should always be the main consideration when dealing with aggression. How would you feel if your dog attacked and maimed another person or killed your neighbor's dog? If your dog poses a threat to others and you cannot guarantee that he will never be able to act on that threat, ask your vet and behaviorist about your options—they can help you find what's best for you and your dog.

## BARKING

Barking is a normal, natural behavior for dogs that communicates a wide range of meanings and emotions, from joy to warning to request to fear. Some breeds tend to be very vocal, barking at every little thing. Others are less inclined to mouth off. Once again, it's useful to know what your dog's ancestors were bred to do to understand why your dog barks a lot or hardly ever. For instance, Shetland Sheepdogs (Shelties) tend to be vocal, especially when at play. As their name tells us, Shelties were (and some still are) used to gather and drive sheep. Because they are small, barking was useful for intimidating and controlling the sheep. Terriers and scent hounds also tend to be vocal because their ancestors used their voices to alert their human hunting partners to the location of prey. Of course, individual dogs within a breed also vary in their tendency to bark.

Most people don't object to a little barking. Some barking is useful—your dog may bark for you to let him in or out or to alert you to a problem. But if your dog barks at everything that moves or barks barks barks for hours on end, he'll no doubt drive you up a wall and irritate your neighbors. He may even bring you a visit from the local authorities, and in some cases, a fine. Barking dogs are a major source of friction among neighbors, so if your dog has been raising a ruckus, let the people who live near you know that you are working on the problem. Even if they haven't complained directly to you about the noise, you can be sure that they've noticed it and probably don't like it, but most people will cut you a little slack if they know you're working to solve the problem. Also, don't leave your dog outdoors when you're away. If you live in an apartment, consider taking your dog to doggy daycare when you're not home to keep him from being a nuisance.

## Management Techniques

If your dog is a problem barker, your first job is to try to figure

### Bark Collars

In our electronic age, it's not surprising that some people look to gadgets to solve dog-training problems. Manufacturers of bark collars (actually anti-bark collars) promise a quick fix for problem barking. The collars administer an automatic punishment—an electrical shock, spray of offensive odor aimed at the dog's nose, or a high-pitched sound. Do they work? Maybe, in some cases. But I've heard dogs bark bark bark while getting zapped and have seen yappy dogs with electrical burns on their necks from their collars. Besides, bark collars treat the symptoms rather than the cause. If your dog barks because he's bored, he'll find something else to do. If he barks because he's afraid or anxious, a bark collar will probably lead to more neurotic behaviors. If he barks because he's territorial or aggressive, he may blame the perceived threat for his discomfort. And obviously, giving your dog an electrical shock or a nose full of noxious odors is definitely not a positive, motivational approach to teaching him how to behave. Prevention, control, and training are better ways to turn down the volume.

*A dog who barks when left alone outside is likely lonely and bored.*

out when and why he barks and to remove the cause, if possible. Then, apply the following techniques to help to manage the problem.

### Don't Leave Your Dog Outside

Does your dog bark when you leave him outside? He's probably lonely and bored—you'd complain, too, if you were shut out by the people you love. He also may be nervous, and with good cause—many dogs every year are stolen from their own yards. All in all, leaving your dog outside for long periods, especially when you aren't home, is not a great idea. He'd be safer, and probably quieter, in the house.

### Exercise Your Dog

Does your dog get enough exercise, or is he barking as a substitute? Is he bored? Many dogs have genes that want jobs but owners who don't give them enough to do. Excessive barking may be an alternative hobby of sorts—and probably not the only one he has if boredom and unused energy are the underlying cause. If you have a high-energy breed or a mixed breed with one or more high-energy ancestors, try increasing his daily exercise to curb barking

*Excessive barking can put you and your dog in the doghouse with your neighbors and possibly with the law.*

and other problem behaviors. Running full tilt for half an hour a day may seem like a lot to you, but for many dogs, that's barely enough to take the edge off.

### Manage Barking Triggers

Does something in particular trigger your dog's barking—a neighbor gardening next door, joggers passing your house, squirrels in the yard? Depending on what the trigger is, you may be able to reduce its impact on your dog or keep him from noticing it.

If your dog barks every time Mrs. Smith works in her garden, explain the situation to Mrs. Smith, and if she is willing, introduce your dog to her. Give Mrs. Smith a treat to give your dog. Be careful how you set up the reward, though. If your dog barks and immediately gets to run to Mrs. Smith for a treat, he'll learn to bark whenever he sees her! Instead, wait until he stops barking, even if just for a few seconds, and then take him out. Or if he's a regular motormouth, take him outside to see Mrs. Smith, but have her withhold the treat until your dog has been there, and quiet, for a few minutes. In other words, reward quiet, not noise.

Teach your dog that having people around is good. (Don't worry—if he has a shred of protectiveness, he'll still warn you if a burglar tries to break in.) Have a friend walk by your yard. If your dog watches quietly, mark and reward him. If he barks, tell him "Sit" or "Settle," and when he's quiet for a few seconds, mark and reward. Gradually increase the length of time he has to stay quiet before earning the reward. Have your friend come a bit closer and repeat the process. You might have the friend reward him for being quiet, although teaching him to expect or take treats from strangers may not be the best idea. In any case, be consistent—don't encourage or ignore his barking one time and discourage it the next. If you follow this process consistently with several different friends, your dog should become more tolerant of people walking near your yard.

Not all triggers can be handled in the way of the previous two examples, of course, but you may be able to keep your dog from noticing them, at least part of the time. If he looks out the front window and barks at squirrels all day, for example, keep him away from that window.

*Dogs with separation anxiety are often problem barkers.*

### *Deal With Emotional Problems*

Dogs with separation anxiety (see "Separation Anxiety") and other emotional problems are often problem barkers. If you suspect that that's the case for your dog and you can't get a handle on the behavior by yourself or with a basic obedience class, ask your vet or obedience instructor to refer you to a qualified behaviorist.

# BEGGING

Do you want to teach your dog to beg? Easy—just feed him something every time you eat, and soon he'll be drooling and staring at you and your friends every time you sit down at the dining table or open a bag of chips in front of the television. Not only will he become an obnoxious pest, but he may develop allergies and tooth decay from eating people food, and he'll almost certainly turn into a four-legged blimp.

*To prevent begging, do not feed your dog from the table.*

## Management Techniques

There are two main ways to keep your dog from begging: Never feed him when you're eating, and never feed him from the table.

### *Never Feed Your Dog When You're Eating*

If you prefer to eat without dog drool on your shoes and "I'm wasting away" eyes staring at you, it's just as easy to teach your dog not to beg—just don't feed him when you are eating. That means nothing. Not a bite, not a lick. Never. If you reward him for begging even just once in a blue moon, he will beg. In fact, as we discussed in Chapter 5, sporadic rewards are more motivating than constant rewards.

### Never Feed Your Dog From the Table

Okay, so you've been talking to my dogs, and you're on to me. I'm not really that tough. I do share little bits of some things with my dogs—a bite of banana, a few bits of popcorn, occasional pizza "bones." But my dogs do not beg when I'm eating, and here's why: I don't share when I or any other human is still eating. So if you want to share (after all, this is your best friend we're talking about), wait until you're finished. Move to another place—across the room or a different room. Use the opportunity to reinforce training—have your pup sit or roll over to earn the treat. Make sure that what you're giving him won't violate any serious dietary restrictions—no corn chips if he's is allergic to corn. Then give him just a tiny taste—you won't feel stingy, and your dog will stay slim, trim, and polite.

## DESTRUCTIVE CHEWING

Chewing is one of life's great joys for many dogs. Puppies chew to relieve the discomfort of loose and emerging teeth when teething. Many dogs chew just because it feels good and because it can relieve stress and redirect potentially destructive energy.

*Puppies need to chew while they are teething, and many dogs continue to enjoy a good chew throughout their lives.*

Chewing on the right things also contributes to your dog's oral health by helping to scrape his teeth clean.

Unfortunately, some dogs will chew anything and everything they can get into their jaws, especially when they are anxious. But as many dog owners know all too well, chewing also can cause a lot of damage to property and can lead to serious, even life-threatening situations for your dog. The good news is that most destructive chewing can be controlled fairly easily if you are proactive.

## Management Techniques

The best management techniques for destructive chewing involve preventive techniques like providing plenty of exercise, confining your dog, and supervising him.

### Exercise Your Dog

Plenty of exercise, coupled with general obedience training, will help to reduce destructive chewing by using up energy and preventing boredom and frustration.

### Confine Your Dog

Confine your dog to a safe area when you can't watch him. A safe room may work if he's not prone to eating woodwork or flooring, but in many cases a crate is a better choice for your dog and your home. Wherever you confine him, be sure that he has one or two nice, "legal" chew toys or bones—like Nylabones—to keep him busy.

I don't advocate locking a dog up for long hours in a crate—four hours at a time should be about the maximum for an adult. (See Chapter 6 on crating puppies.) If you have to be gone longer than that on a regular basis, consider hiring or bartering with someone to come and let him out once or twice a day. A secure (locked) outdoor dog run with shelter may be a reasonable alternative if your dog is not a barker and if he has a doggy door or other access to a safe, comfortable indoor space. Leaving your dog outdoors subjects him to potential dangers, including being teased, poisoned, injured, or stolen, so carefully consider whether that is a safe option for your situation.

### Supervise Your Dog

When you're with your dog, keep an eye on him. I confess that one time I was careless about watching my Lab, Raja. He lay at my feet chewing away, and I assumed he had his bone. By the time I actually checked, he had the heel pretty well off a pair of my dress shoes. You can be sure I checked what he had after that! If your dog does pick up something he shouldn't have, take it from him gently and give him one of his own toys. (See the "Give" and Leave It" sections in Chapter 8 to train your dog to give things to you).

### Be Patient

Be patient. It may be obvious to you that your leather shoes are off-limits while rawhide toys are "legal," but to your dog they're all just animal hide, and the shoes smell like his favorite thing—you! Put belongings you really don't want chewed out of reach, supervise your dog, give him what he needs, and you'll keep chewing in the realm of canine pleasure rather than human pain.

# DIGGING

Many dogs will dig in the ground on occasion, but some breeds are born to dig. Terriers and Dachshunds, for example, originated as working and hunting dogs who located vermin and prey animals in their dens and dug them out. For dogs with terrier

*Many dogs enjoy digging, and for some breeds, the urge to dig is as natural as breathing or eating.*

If you amend your garden soil with certain products, you may inadvertently encourage your dog to dig. Fish emulsion, bonemeal, and blood meal, for instance, smell like animal parts (because they are), and your dog may dig to find the rest of the body. (He also may roll on the spot to anoint himself with eau de dead fish or cow manure.) Be careful about using products in your garden that might encourage your dog to dig.

or Dachshund blood (and some others), digging is as natural as breathing or eating. Dogs dig for other reasons, too. Some bury bones and treasure for safekeeping, or they dig for things they smell under the ground. Some excavate tunnels to escape the confines of a fence or wall. On a hot day, your dog may dig out a nice, cool "bed" for himself. If he is bored or full of energy he can't spend elsewhere, he may dig for something to do. Besides, digging is just fun!

## Management Techniques

A determined digger can wreak havoc in your yard in no time. But how can you stop him? You can keep your dog from digging altogether with preventive techniques like supervision, the use of barriers and repellants, and energy channeling. Or you can allow "appropriate" digging by redirecting it to a more suitable spot. Both approaches require some effort and planning, but if you don't want potholes in your petunias, you will have to do something.

### Supervise Your Dog

You can supervise your dog whenever he's outdoors, but for most people, that's not very practical. After all, even if you're in the yard with him, your dog could dig a hole under the hollyhocks while you're watering the wisteria. Other preventive techniques may work better.

### Use Barriers and Repellants

You also can try to discourage your digger with barriers and repellants of various kinds. For instance, if your dog has a favorite digging spot, try filling or covering his hole with rocks, a flower pot, or some other physical barrier that he can't move. If he digs under a fence, try sinking a few inches (cm) of chicken wire or chain link fencing vertically along the fence line. If he burrows into the soft earth around plants, you can bury chicken wire horizontally under a layer of soil to block his path. Check the fence line frequently to be sure that he hasn't started a new project.

A number of products are supposed to discourage digging. Some might thwart some dogs, but most don't work very well and a few are downright dangerous. Home remedies like black and cayenne pepper sprinkled on top of the soil lose their strength quickly and don't always work. Mothballs repel animals, but they are highly toxic for you and your dog and not a good choice. Commercial products also vary widely in their effectiveness, and most are probably not worth the money. Even if these digging repellants do discourage your dog from digging, they do not give him an alternative outlet for the energy and drive that motivated him to dig in the first place. If he quits digging, he will probably find something else to do, and chances are you won't like that activity either.

### Channel Your Dog's Energy

Consider channeling your dog's energy into other activities. Practice basic obedience skills and tricks, play retrieving and hide-and-seek games, or participate in other canine sports for fun or competition. If he's a member of an eligible breed, you might consider taking your dog to earth events (see Chapter 10) so that he can show off his underground talents!

### Redirect the Digging

If your dog is a persistent digger, you might have more success redirecting his digging than trying to prevent it. You don't need much space to give him a place of his own to excavate. Pick a spot with loose sand or sandy soil, or build your dog a sandbox. (Sand is cleaner than clay or loam.) Put up a barrier to control flying sand or dirt, and be sure that the sand is deep enough to let your dog really dig into it. To encourage him to dig in that spot, bury a treat or a toy, then show your dog the place and encourage him to dig for buried treasure. Repeat the process over a few days. Supervise your dog whenever he's outdoors until you feel he's reliable. If you see him digging elsewhere in the yard, calmly and quietly say, "Leave it," and take him to his digging spot.

## HOUSETRAINING PROBLEMS

Although the occasional dog is by nature a slob, most housetraining problems result because a dog has been conditioned to live in filth, because he was never fully housetrained in the first place, or because he has a physical problem that prevents him from eliminating properly.

## Management Techniques

If your dog is having trouble with housetraining and came from

a puppy mill or was rescued, he may need to learn to appreciate cleanliness. If this is not an issue with your dog, he may just need his housetraining refreshed, or he may have a physical problem that requires veterinary attention.

### Condition Your Dog to Cleanliness

Dogs by nature prefer to urinate and defecate away from where they sleep and eat, but dogs (especially puppies) who are kept in dirty surroundings, living in their own waste, become indifferent to filth. Puppies from puppy mills and dogs rescued from bad situations often fall into this category. With patient training and supervision, most can eventually be reconditioned to appreciate cleanliness by following strict housetraining procedures (see Chapter 6) and by keeping them and their living quarters scrupulously clean until new habits form.

### Refresh Your Dog's Housetraining

Incomplete training is probably the biggest reason for potty problems in dogs. In short, don't give your dog more responsibility than he can handle. If he is not completely reliable, don't give him the run of the house, and don't let him loose even in one room when you cannot supervise him. Small dogs in particular often need more time to develop reliable habits. Don't expect your dog to be housetrained according to some arbitrary schedule. He may be trained in ten days or it may take ten months. Review "Housetraining" in Chapter 6, and stick to a regular routine as long as necessary. Help your dog get it right.

### See Your Vet

Physical problems, including diseases, infections, parasites, and other factors, can cause diarrhea and loss of bowel and urinary tract control that make it difficult or impossible for your dog to control his elimination. If housetraining takes longer than you think it should, or if your dog breaks housetraining after being reliable, speak to your vet.

*Speak to your vet if you suspect that your dog may have a housetraining problem—she can rule out or diagnose a physical cause.*

# JUMPING UP

A dog who jumps on people uninvited is at best a nuisance and at worst a hazard to life and limb. Children, elderly people, and people with physical problems can be seriously injured by a dog who doesn't keep his feet where they belong.

But why do dogs jump up in the first place? Jumping up may be partly instinctive. If you watch dogs interacting, especially puppies and older dogs, you will see that the young or subordinate animal will lick the adult or more dominant animal's mouth and chin. This is a behavior that signals submission, and the dominant (or adult) dog recognizes the licking as polite and socially appropriate. So it's natural that your dog, especially when he's young, wants to lick your mouth—he wants to tell you that he respects you and acknowledges you as his leader. Puppies often have to jump or stand up against the bigger dog to lick. They will behave the same way with people and are often rewarded for jumping up or climbing someone's leg by being picked up and cuddled.

Naturally, unless your puppy is taught differently, he will continue to jump up into adulthood. A behavior that seems cute in a roly-poly puppy isn't so cute when that puppy grows up, but by that time he's been taught that people pay attention when he jumps up. Of course, by the time your dog is an adolescent, you're probably shouting and shoving him when he jumps. You think you're telling him to stay off, but he thinks "Hey, my human is paying attention to me, and playing. What fun!"

*If your dog is not reliably housetrained, don't give him the run of the house. As this Bulldog shows, baby gates are useful for restricting your dog to certain rooms.*

## Management Techniques

To teach your dog to stop jumping up, plan ahead, think carefully about what behaviors you reward, and then be consistent. If you have a young puppy, now is the time to begin teaching him not to jump up. Remember, no matter what you do, your puppy learns something—but is it something you want him to learn? More to the point, is it something you will want him to do when he's much, much bigger? If you pick him up, you are teaching him that jumping gets him a cuddle. If you push him down gently and pet him, you teach him that jumping gets him nice attention from your hands. If you get all excited and push him away, he thinks you're playing, unless you hurt him, in which case he learns not to trust you. So, think about the lesson you are teaching before you do anything. If your dog is older and is in the habit of jumping, it's time to retrain him. Two approaches have worked for me: Ignore the jumper, or give the jumper something else to do.

### Ignore the Jumping Behavior

Some dogs quickly learn to stop jumping up if you completely ignore them when they do. Whether you can ignore your dog will depend in part on how big and rough he is, of course. But behavior that is not rewarded tends to disappear, so ignoring your dog's pleas for attention and rewarding him when he keeps his feet on the ground will eventually discourage him from jumping.

For this approach to work, you must plan ahead. Wear old clothes whenever your dog has access to you. When he jumps up, don't say anything. Simply fold your arms across your chest and look up. He may continue to jump for a while, especially if you've been in the habit of pushing him down and generally being more interesting than you are when you ignore him. If you wait it out, though,

*Regardless of size, a dog who follows his instinct to jump on people is a nuisance and potentially dangerous. Teach your dog not to jump up unless you invite him.*

he'll realize that you turn into a boring lump when he jumps up on you, and he'll quit. When he has his feet back on the ground, mark that behavior and reward him with some calm attention. If he gets excited and jumps up again, turn back into a boring lump. You will have to be patient and consistent, but if you are, your dog will learn not to jump on you. This approach is especially effective with young puppies who have not yet learned that jumping up makes you pay attention.

### Have Your Dog Perform an Alternate Behavior

Another approach that works well if your dog has had some other training is to give him something else to do—like the *sit*,     *down*, or *settle*. Ideally you should anticipate his jumping up and give the command before he does, then mark and reward the correct behavior. The main problem with this approach is that your dog has to know the command you give him or he can't respond to it. Then again, you plan to teach him those commands anyway, so think of the jumping problem as motivation for you.

To transfer the lesson to keeping your dog off other people, you will need your leash. When greeting someone, keep control of your dog with the leash and ask the person not to touch or talk to your dog until he is doing what you told him (probably a *sit*). When he sits, the person may pet him or even give him a treat. If he starts to jump again, they should back off and ignore him until he's sitting again. If that isn't feasible because of the person's size, age, physical condition, or lack of cooperation, use your leash to keep your dog away from the person and have him sit or settle.

If your dog doesn't respond to the alternate command and continues to jump up, put his leash on so that you have more control. Remain calm, shorten the leash enough so that your dog has very little room to maneuver, and return to "teaching mode," treating him as if he's never heard of the *sit* command. Lure him into the *sit* if you must, and mark and reward him as if it were a whole new command. In some ways it is—it's one thing for him to sit when everything is calm and quiet but another thing when you just get home from work or Aunt Mabel, who always gives your dog a biscuit, comes to visit.

Children often react to nips by screaming, pushing the puppy away, running, and getting excited. Puppies react to such behavior, which they interpret as play, by nipping, chasing, and jumping up. Things can get out of hand very quickly, and your puppy or child can end up frightened or injured or both. All interaction between your puppy and children should be supervised by a responsible adult who is able to intervene immediately. Don't let unsupervised interaction spoil what should be one of the most wonderful relationships in

# MOUTHING OR BITING

Why does your puppy (or dog) insist on putting his mouth on everyone? One reason is that he uses his mouth, along with his nose, to explore the world, much as we use our fingers. A more important reason is that he uses his mouth to interact socially with other dogs, and he must be taught that people generally don't appreciate the finer points of licking, mouthing, nuzzling, nibbling, and jaw-sparring. Besides, we don't have the fur to protect our skin, so we're much too vulnerable to those sharp little puppy teeth.

Some dogs, particularly if they have genes that tell them to carry things constantly (like the retrieving breeds have), never outgrow the urge to take hands in their mouths. It's not a good habit to allow, though. Even if your dog is gentle, people often interpret hand mouthing as an attempt to bite, and if a person jerks away, your dog's tooth could cause injury and get both of you in big trouble.

## Management Techniques

All puppies and dogs should learn that chomping down on people is never allowed, not even in play. And don't worry—in the unlikely event that you ever need your dog to protect you, good everyday mouth manners won't stop him. If he has any protective instinct (and most dogs do), he will know if you are in danger. But he doesn't need to refine his skills on your wrist.

### *Redirect the Behavior*

One simple but effective way to stop nipping is to replace the attractive body part with something he is allowed to chew. When he takes your hand or ankle in his mouth, gently offer him a chew toy—Nylabone makes some suitable ones—and pet him and praise him for doing something good. He'll learn that hands are gentle things for belly and ear rubs, not organic chewies.

### *Ignore Your Dog*

If your dog still mouths and bites, try Plan B—you may want to wear old clothes, including closed-toe shoes and long pants, for this one. When he chomps on you, say "Ouch!" and then stand up and ignore him. If he jumps up, continue to ignore him—maybe he will learn two lessons at once! Your hands are out of reach, so he may go for your ankles or your pants. If he is in a safe place, leave him briefly (no more than a minute), then calmly return and play gently, encouraging him again to play with you but chew on the chew toy.

### Try a Spray-On Product

There is also a Plan C for the really determined dog—make yourself taste bad. You can purchase a bitter apple spray-on product that tastes terrible. (Wear old clothes, or test a discrete spot to be sure that your clothes don't stain.) Menthol vapor rubs also discourage chewing and licking. If you use these on your hands, be sure to wash well before you handle food.

Speaking of your hands—they should never be used to hit your puppy for mouthing (or anything else). Hitting will not teach the lesson you intend. If your puppy is bold and confident, he may think

*Teach your puppy to bite and chew on his own toys and treats, not your ankles and hands.*

you're playing and nip even more. If he thinks you're attempting to hurt him (which you are), he may react by biting, which is very different from play nipping and potentially a serious problem for both of you. If your pup is sensitive or submissive, hitting him could lead to other problem behaviors—submissive urination, cringing from hands coming toward him, and reluctance to come when called, among others. A frightened puppy may become a "fear biter" who tries to defend himself from perceived threats by biting.

## Aggressive Biting

Aggressive biting is completely different from normal mouthing. If your puppy (or dog) bares his teeth or snaps at any person, ask your veterinarian or obedience instructor for a referral, and talk to a dog trainer or behaviorist who is qualified to evaluate the behavior and to deal with aggression. Don't wait—if your puppy is just very pushy, you must get control as soon as possible. If he's showing true aggression, it will not get better on its own and could escalate, so get professional help.

*Teach your dog from the start that you control the resources he wants.*

### Let Your Dog Rest

Another point to be aware of concerning puppies—a tired puppy is usually a good puppy, but sometimes exhaustion makes for silly, out-of-control behavior. Like human children, puppies aren't always sensible about going to bed. If your pup has been awake for quite a while, and his play seems a bit frantic and crazy, put him in his crate, give him a treat and a chew toy, and let him rest. He may protest for a minute or two, then sleep like an angel.

## RESOURCE GUARDING

An old joke revises the Golden Rule thus: "He who has the gold rules." We can apply the same principle to our relationship with our dogs, changing "gold" to "resources." A resource in this sense is anything that has value to the dog—food, a toy, a dog bed, the couch, even a person. One of the most common—and most dangerous— problem behaviors seen in pet dogs is what behaviorists call resource guarding—an animal's attempt to control a resource and prevent other dogs or people from having access to it.

## Management Techniques

Resource guarding can escalate to a dangerous level of aggression if ignored or encouraged. Some breeds are more prone than others to resource guarding, but you can teach most dogs not to guard, particularly if you start when they're young.

### Take Control of the Resource

At the first sign that your puppy or dog is aggressively guarding something, take control of that resource. (Be aware, though, that dogs do growl and tug and tease each other when playing—be sure that what you're seeing is not just normal "play talk.") Teach the *give* and *leave it* commands. (See Chapter 8)

Food is a resource, and your dog may try to exert some control over his food by guarding it from other animals and people, especially children. If that happens, you must take complete control of your dog's food. Teach him to sit or lie down and stay there, even after you set his food down, until you release him. (Put his leash on for control if necessary.) Dole his dinner out to him a bite at a time at first, and have him earn each bite by obeying a command—like *sit* or *down*. The idea is to remind him that you, not he, hold the key to the larder. When he is behaving himself a bite at a time, put part of his dinner in his bowl, and set it down. When he has eaten that portion, pick up his bowl and give him a little more. While he's eating, have him stop and sit or lie down. Lift his bowl, hold it for a moment, and then put it down and release him. If he growls or otherwise threatens you, be very cautious. If possible, remove the food completely. If your dog is behaving himself, have your child put him in a *sit* or *down-stay*, give him his food, and release him. An adult should supervise all food-related interaction between child and dog and intervene if necessary.

### Where to Find a Qualified Canine Behaviorist

If your dog has problem behaviors that don't respond to regular obedience training, or if he displays aggression toward people or other animals, a qualified canine behaviorist may be able to help. Be careful who you choose— anyone can claim to be a dog trainer or behaviorist. To find a qualified person, ask your veterinarian for a referral, or go to www.inch.com/~dogs/behaviorists.html. Then ask lots of questions, and check references.

The same regime will work with other resources. Remember—your dog doesn't pay the bills, so he's not in charge. If he gets too possessive of a particular toy, take it away for a while. If he thinks he owns the couch or a chair and growls at other pets or people who come near it, he should lose his furniture privileges. The same goes for your bed. Don't worry that your dog will get mad at you or not love you for limiting his privileges. In fact, if anything he will love and respect you more for being a fair but firm pack leader.

### Get Professional Help

If your dog is already in the habit of guarding resources, and especially if he is threatening to bite or has bitten, get help immediately from a qualified trainer or behaviorist.

# SEPARATION ANXIETY

Separation anxiety refers to a condition that causes a dog to become extremely worried and agitated when left alone. Separation anxiety can cause a range of behaviors ranging from mild to severe.

*A dog with signs of separation anxiety should be secured in a safe place when he must spend time alone. This Labrador Retriever feels safe and comfortable in his crate.*

A dog may bark, whine, or howl, or pace the floor for hours. He may destroy furniture and other objects or chew himself raw. He may salivate excessively or vomit, and even though he's normally housetrained, he may defecate or urinate as a nervous response to stress.

## Management Techniques

Effective treatment for separation anxiety requires time and patience. In extreme cases, your veterinarian can prescribe an anti-anxiety medication to calm your dog and break the behavioral pattern, but drugs are not the best long-term solution in most cases. Behavior modification should accompany any drug therapy and is sometimes effective by itself.

*A dog with separation anxiety becomes worried and agitated when left alone.*

### Keep Your Dog (and Your Belongings) Safe

The first step in managing a dog with separation anxiety is to be sure that your dog and your belongings are safe in your absence. Many dogs feel safer when confined to a crate (which is a cozy den to most dogs), so crate train your dog (see Chapter 6) and put him in his crate when you aren't home. Give him a couple of safe chew toys so that he'll have something to do. If your dog is prone to ripping things up when he's anxious, be cautious about leaving anything he can rip up and swallow, including bedding, in his reach. A few dogs panic when crated and will tear up the crate or injure themselves trying to get out. If your dog is like that, you might want to try a slow process of teaching him to accept the crate (see Chapter 6), and find an alternate place to secure him when you're not with him.

### Teach Your Dog to Settle and Stay

Teach your dog to settle and stay (see Chapter 7), and have him stay in one place for varying lengths of time while you're home but not necessarily right next to him. This will begin to teach him that he doesn't have to cling to you to be safe and that you will come back. Reward him for staying and becoming relaxed, and have him

*Love and patience are essential for solving problem behaviors, but sometimes professional help is also needed.*

spend varying lengths of time in his crate (or wherever you confine him) while you're home so that he learns that it's a safe place whether you're there or not.

### Find Your Dog a Comfortable Environment

Try to figure out what environment is most comfortable and relaxing for your dog. If he likes to look out the window, put his crate where he can watch the world go by. If he's happier hidden away, put the crate in a more private location. The sound of a radio or television—especially soft music or talk shows—reassures many dogs. (But beware of the shows with a lot of angry people yelling and screaming.)

If your dog is not a destroyer who is likely to swallow something that he shouldn't, he might be comforted by something that smells like you—an old sweatshirt, for instance. One of my dogs used to take one of my walking shoes to his bed when I was gone.

### Keep Your Comings and Goings Low-Key

Don't make a fuss when you leave or come home (or when you leave your dog with your groomer or vet). If you make separating a big deal, your dog will be convinced that he's right to worry. When you are nearly ready to leave home, put your dog in his crate so that he can relax before you leave. Give him something special that he gets only when you're about to leave—a chew toy or hollow bone stuffed with soft cheese or peanut butter and kibble please most dogs. Once he's in his crate, ignore him, and when you're ready to leave, do so with no further fuss. When you return, again, don't make a fuss. Leave your dog in his crate for a few minutes, and when he's relaxed, calmly let him out. Show him that your comings and goings are no big deal.

### Determine Your Dog's Anxiety Threshold

Try to figure out when it is that your dog becomes anxious. Does he raise a ruckus as soon as he's locked up? When you walk out the door? An hour later? Then begin a reconditioning process by leaving him alone and returning before he reaches his "anxiety limit," if possible. If he starts to bark when you've been gone two minutes, stand outside the door for one minute and then come back in. If he stayed calm, mark and reward while he is still in his crate. If he didn't do so well, come in and ignore him until he calms down, then repeat the process, maybe for a shorter period. Even if you have to leave him for longer periods most days, these exercises repeated on weekends and in the evenings will teach your dog that sometimes you won't be gone so long, and in any case, you'll be back and he will be safe until you are.

### Give Your Dog a Midday Break

If you must be gone frequently for more than four hours at a time, you might want to pay or barter with someone to give your dog a midday break. Make sure that your dog is comfortable with the person and that the person is aware of the procedures you are using to help your dog through his problem.

How quickly a problem behavior can be corrected depends on many factors—your dog's age, how long he's had the bad habit, why he does what he does, and how you and other people respond to the problem. Most problem behaviors can be controlled—if not eliminated—but some can be very challenging. If you can't fix a problem on your own, have your veterinarian or a qualified animal behaviorist evaluate your dog's situation and recommend a treatment plan. And be sure to train your dog in the basics if you haven't yet. General obedience training will build your dog's sense of security and trust, and that can go a long way toward preventing bad behavior.

# Chapter 10

# FUN

## With Your Well-Trained Dog

ogs are probably the most adaptable of all domestic animals. Other animals share our lives and give us a lot of pleasure, but your dog is the one who will accompany you wherever let him. In this final chapter, I'll suggest some sports and activities that you and your well-trained dog might enjoy, as well as show you a few tricks to tuck into your dog's fur. This is just a sampling of the many opportunities that exist to team up with your canine partner, so whether you want to work, play, or just unwind, there's something out there for the two of you.

## THE AKC CANINE GOOD CITIZEN® (CGC) CERTIFICATE

The Canine Good Citizen (CGC) testing and certification program was developed by the American Kennel Club (AKC) as a way to promote basic training and responsible dog care and to reward well-behaved dogs—and well-behaved dog owners! During the CGC test, the dog performs a series of ten subtests in an environment that simulates some of the conditions you might encounter when out in the community with your dog. The evaluators consider each dog's basic temperament and response to people, strange dogs, loud noises, and visual distractions. The dog is also expected to respond to basic obedience commands and must be reasonably clean and well groomed and vaccinated against rabies as required by law. Your dog must pass all ten of the subtests to earn the official designation of Canine Good Citizen.

During the test, your dog must wear a properly fitted buckle or slip (choke) collar made of leather, fabric, or chain and must be kept on leash at all times. You are also asked to bring your dog's own brush or comb for use during one of the subtests, as well as written proof of his up-to-date rabies vaccination. (A rabies tag will not be accepted as proof of vaccination because it doesn't identify the dog.)

This is a test of "good citizenship," so in addition to performing the subtests, the dog is required to act as you'd expect a good citizen to act. Therefore, any dog who growls,

*A well-trained, well-mannered dog is a delight.*

snaps, bites, attacks, or tries to attack another dog or a person will be dismissed from the test area and will not be awarded the CGC certification.

If your aspiring good citizen doesn't pass the test, don't be discouraged. The CGC test gives you a chance to see what you still need to work on. Remember, learning takes time, and transferring learned behaviors to strange new environments takes even longer. A testing environment is stimulating and stressful—new sights and sounds, new people and dogs. And make no mistake—if you have a little test anxiety (as most people do), your dog will know it and become anxious, too. So go home, keep training, love your dog, and try again.

## SPORTS AND ACTIVITIES

Obedience classes and training may be simply a means to an end for you—a way to teach your dog to be a well-behaved companion. That's as worthwhile a pursuit any! But if you're like a lot of people, you may find that you really enjoy the time you spend training your dog and associating with like-minded dog lovers. If you want to keep training beyond basic good manners, there are plenty of activities to choose from, and there's undoubtedly at least one that will suit you and your pooch. Whatever you choose, training will strengthen the bond between you and your dog and channel your dog's physical and mental energy in positive directions.

## Sports for All Dogs

One of the nice things about dog sports is that you can choose to participate just for fun, to earn titles, or to become highly competitive. Just don't be blinded by the fancy ribbons and titles—remember that it was love for your dog that got you there in the first place. The time we spend in the company of these loving, forgiving creatures is the best prize of all.

### The American Kennel Club Canine Good Citizen® Test

To earn the designation AKC Canine Good Citizen (CGC), your dog must pass each of the following 10 tests.

1. Accept a friendly stranger, who will approach, shake your hand, and speak to you, as might happen on a walk. Your dog must remain beside you without acting shy or resentful.

2. Sit politely while the friendly stranger pets his head and body. Once again, your dog must not act shy or resentful.

3. Your dog must be clean and well groomed and appear to be well cared for. He must allow someone other than you to comb or brush his coat and gently check his ears and front feet.

4. Your dog must walk quietly on leash while making several turns and stopping with you at least twice.

5. Your dog must walk with you past and among at least three strangers, showing that he is polite and under control in public.

6. Your dog must demonstrate some basic training by sitting, lying down, and staying on command.

7. Your dog must stay where you tell him and then come when you call him from 10 feet (3.0 m) away.

8. Your dog must walk with you to approach and meet another person with a dog and must show no more than casual interest in the other dog.

9. Your dog must stay calm when faced with two common distractions (for example, a falling object, a jogger, a bicycle passing by).

10. Your dog must stay calm and polite when left with the evaluator while you go out of sight for three minutes.

### Agility

Agility, which you may have seen on television if not in person, requires a dog to negotiate a course of jumps, tunnels, and other obstacles in the proper order and within a specified time limit. Even if you aren't interested in competing or earning titles on your dog, practicing agility with simple homemade equipment is a fun way to reinforce your bond with your dog, run off some of his energy, and just plain have a great time. Just be sure that his bones are mature (see Chapter 3) before training on jumps or weave poles, use safe equipment, and don't push him beyond his ability or endurance.

If you want to compete, several organizations sponsor agility

*Agility has skyrocketed in popularity over the past decade.*

competition at all levels, from novice through advanced. Any sound, healthy dog, from tiny toy breeds to large sight hounds, can participate in agility, but active, athletic dogs in particular excel at the sport.

## Flyball

If excitement is your game, try flyball, a sport in which dogs run relay races in teams of four. Each team member zooms down a lane over a series of four hurdles and hits a peddle to release a tennis ball from a spring-loaded box. The dog grabs the ball and races back to the starting line.

Like agility, the dogs who excel in flyball are fast, athletic dogs, regardless of size.

## Obedience

The sport of obedience is designed to demonstrate and test teamwork between dog and handler, as well as the ability of the dog to learn and perform useful tasks, such as basic obedience commands.

With modern motivational training methods, dogs of every shape and size can and do earn obedience titles at all levels.

*If you enjoy a challenge and the company of other dog-lovers, you and your dog may enjoy a competitive dog sport. This Shetland Sheepdog is practicing for the obedience ring.*

## Rally-O

A new dog sport hit the scene in 2001 when the Association of Pet Dog Trainers (APDT) began its Rally Obedience Program. The AKC followed suit in January 2005, and rally has quickly become extremely popular. More informal and less rigid and demanding than competition obedience or agility, rally requires the dog-and-handler team to negotiate a predetermined course of stations at which they demonstrate specific skills. If you are just beginning to compete with your dog, or if your dog is unable to perform in agility or advanced obedience due to age or physical limitation, rally may be just what you're looking for.

Any reasonably healthy dog can participate in rally-o.

### Tracking

Tracking, in which your dog follows a specified scent trail with his powerful nose, is a wonderful low-stress way to spend active time outdoors, although it does require that dog and handler be fit enough to walk long distances over sometimes rough terrain.

Most dogs can track, although tiny dogs may need some help getting over large obstacles and may not be able to track in very cold weather. Also, brachycephalic—pug-nosed—dogs are more prone to overheating in warm weather.

### Other Sports

In addition to the sports listed in this section, you may be interested in a sport that tests the talents for which your dog's ancestors were developed—like herding livestock; finding, flushing, or retrieving birds or other game; running in pursuit of a lure; "going to ground" after varmints; performing water rescues; pulling loads; and so on. The Internet and your local library can provide the information you need to get your dog and yourself moving.

*Tracking is a fun way to put your dog's powerful nose to work.*

**Learn More About Canine Activities**

You can learn more about various kinds of canine competition from the following organizations:

- American Herding Breeds Association (AHBA)
  www.ahba-herding.org
- American Kennel Club (AKC)
  www.akc.org
- American Mixed Breed Obedience Registry (AMBOR)
  www.amborusa.com
- Delta Society Pet Partners Programs
  www.deltasociety.org
- North American Dog Agility Council (NADAC)
  www.nadac.com
- North American Flyball Association (NAFA)
  www.flyball.org
- Therapy Dogs Inc.
  www.therapydogs.com
- Therapy Dogs International, Inc. (TDI)
  www.tdi-dog.org
- United Kennel Club (UKC)
  www.ukcdogs.com
- United States Dog Agility Association (USDAA)
  www.usdaa.com

## Animal-Assisted Activities and Therapy

If you like to volunteer and can commit to a regular schedule, if your dog is obedient and well behaved, and if you and your dog both enjoy meeting all sorts of people, you might be interested in working as a therapy dog team. What will your dog do as a therapy dog? He may spend the time sitting or lying quietly while being petted, or he might be more active as he entertains people or "assists" a professional person. Clients will often try to do things for a sweet dog that they won't do for a human being—walk a dog down the hall, move an arm to brush a dog or throw a toy, and so on. Children especially respond to dogs, and programs in which kids with reading difficulties read to a dog or in which kids talk to a dog about their experiences or problems are highly successful. My dogs have worked as "motivators" for people in physical rehabilitation and have listened to countless books read by kids with reading difficulties.

Whatever your dog's role in a therapy setting, it's absolutely critical that he like people and be comfortable in new, sometimes strange, situations. He must also have enough obedience training to be reliable.

### What's a Therapy Dog?

The term "therapy dog" is used in general terms to refer to a dog who works, usually as a volunteer with his owner, in two different types of settings. A dog involved in animal-assisted

*If your dog is obedient and well behaved, he may make a good therapy dog.*

activities (AAA) visits people in a variety of situations—nursing homes, hospitals, hospices, shelters, schools, and literacy and reading programs are a few of the possibilities. Although the visits may be highly beneficial, they do not constitute medical therapy because no professional therapist is involved with the visit, and no formal evaluation is made of the dog's impact on people's progress or treatment. In contrast, the dog and handler involved in animal-assisted therapy (AAT) work with a professional therapist, teacher, or doctor who directs activities and keeps records so that the concrete benefits of the visits can be evaluated.

### Certifying Organizations

Several organizations certify therapy dogs, providing education, testing, and insurance coverage for their members. Some local organizations also certify therapy dogs, but the value

Some people confuse therapy dogs with service dogs. Service dogs undergo intensive training to assist people as guide dogs for the blind, hearing dogs for the deaf, general assistance dogs, and so on. Some service dogs are trained to alert their owners to impending seizures and other life-endangering conditions. The Americans with Disabilities Act (ADA) gives service dogs full legal access to virtually every place their owners can go. Although they unquestionably have profound effects on the people they touch physically and emotionally, therapy dogs do not have to undergo extensive, specialized training, and they have no special legal rights.

of certification by such groups varies widely, so be careful. Many dog-and-handler teams work alone or with one or two other teams, which may include dogs, cats, or other animals. Some work as part of a group. If you prefer company, check with local hospitals, nursing homes, libraries, and other institutions, or with your local obedience and kennel clubs, many of which have therapy groups.

### The Emotional Ups and Downs of Therapy Work

The rewards of therapy work can be both subtle and profound. I have watched my dog Reno seek out an autistic child week after week and patiently persist until the child responded. I have seen my dog Teddy lay his head in the lap of a 93-year-old stroke victim humiliated to tears by her body's betrayal. He stopped her tears and inspired her to try, try again to regain control of her ball-throwing arm. Those are moments to make your heart soar.

Other moments can be difficult to deal with. In many situations, you and your dog will work with people who are approaching the ends of their lives or who have suffered deep physical and/ or emotional trauma. You will know if the stress is more than you care to handle, but you also need to be alert to subtle signs that your dog is unhappy. Some dogs like certain kinds of visits but not others. Several of my dogs have worked with special needs children, but my Holly was very nervous in that environment—she knew that these babies had problems, and she didn't know what to do about it. She was delighted, though, to visit regular classrooms, hospitals, and nursing homes. So pay attention to your dog, and even if you both handle the stresses well, you may need a break from time to time or a change of scenery.

### Target Training Required

Targeting is used to teach some of the tricks in this chapter, so if you haven't yet taught your dog to go to and touch a target, do that now. (See "Touch the Target" in Chapter 8.)

## TRICK TRAINING

Tricks are lots of fun for both you and your dog, but like all forms of play, they are more. Trick training engages your dog's mind and relieves boredom, which will almost certainly help to prevent mischief. Another benefit is that the more you teach your dog, the easier it becomes for him to learn new things—and you will become a better trainer, too. If your dog makes therapy visits, tricks are great entertainment, and if you train for advanced forms of competition, tricks can be used to play with your dog and relieve tension. So let's get tricky!

## Sit Pretty

*Sit pretty* or *sit up* is an old standard and one of the cutest tricks your dog can learn. What's more endearing than a dog sitting balanced on his hips, body perpendicular to the ground, paws folded demurely against his chest? This is an easy trick to teach and most dogs can do it (although the occasional canine seems to have "spaghetti spine" and can't hold the position).

### *Prerequisites and Equipment*

Your dog should know the *sit* command, and the *stay* command is helpful although not absolutely necessary. You need treats, your marker, and if your dog is prone to walking away in the middle of a lesson, a leash.

# TROUBLESHOOTING
## *Sit Pretty*

*Rowdy can't balance on his butt.*
Some dogs are definitely more talented at sitting pretty than others, but most can learn to balance for at least a few seconds. If necessary, help him balance by letting him lean his paws against your arm while you encourage him to reach upward for the treat.

*Rowdy stands on his hind legs to reach for the treat.*
Keep the treat lower, just above his muzzle, so that he doesn't feel that he needs to reach so far.

*Tricks are fun for you to teach and for your dog to perform.*

### *Teaching* Sit Pretty *Step By Step*

1. Tell your dog to sit. Hold a treat just above his nose and slowly move it up and very slightly toward his back. Tell him "Sit pretty."
2. As he lifts his paws off the ground, mark and treat. Be sure that you mark and treat only when his front feet are off the ground and his fanny is on the ground.
3. If he balances and holds the pose easily, you can increase the time he has to sit pretty to earn the marker and reward. If he has a little trouble balancing, just take the process more slowly.
4. As he gets the idea, wean the lure away, but continue to mark the behavior and reward your dog for success.

## Spin and Twirl

Another very cute pair of tricks are the *spin* and *twirl*, in which your dog makes a full circle in one direction or the other. You can help your dog distinguish clockwise from counterclockwise by giving each direction a different name—I use "spin" for clockwise and "twirl" for counterclockwise. Just make sure that you can remember which is which!

### *Prerequisites and Equipment*

Targeting is helpful but not required. You need treats and a target stick if you are using one.

### *Teaching Spin Step By Step*

*Spin* and *twirl* can be taught by several methods, so pick the one that suits you and your dog. If your dog is a natural spinner and twirler, you may be able to capture the behavior by marking and rewarding him when he makes a circle one way or the other. (See "Capturing" in Chapter 5.) You also can use targeting or luring to teach these tricks.

If you are using a target:

1. Warm your dog up by having him touch the target a few times, and mark and reward each time he does.
2. Then very slowly move the target parallel to your dog's right side and toward his tail.
3. Tell him "Touch," and keep the target just beyond his reach.
4. When he has followed it all the way around to the right, let him touch it, then mark and reward.
5. When he has the idea and will follow the target quickly all the

# TROUBLESHOOTING

## *Spin*

*Rowdy doesn't follow the target or lure all the way around at first.*

Teach him in increments, maybe a quarter circle at first, then a half circle, three-quarters, and full.

way around, add the *spin* command, telling him "Spin, touch." When he spins reliably with both commands, begin to use "spin" alone.

6. When he does that reliably, remove the target, but continue to mark and reward the correct response.

If you are luring instead of targeting:

1. Show your dog the treat in your hand, then slowly move your hand with the treat parallel to your dog's right side and toward his tail, luring him around in a circle.
2. When he follows the lure reliably and fairly quickly, add the command "Spin."

### *Teaching* Twirl *Step by Step*

Teach *twirl* the same way that you taught *spin*, but turn your dog to his left (counterclockwise) instead. Do five repetitions of *spin*, then five repetitions of *twirl* in a session, then repeat, and then go do something else.

When your dog will spin and twirl reliably, you can begin giving each command randomly, mixing them up and helping your dog clarify the distinction between the two.

## Shake Hands and Paws Off

Because shaking hands isn't a natural canine behavior, most dogs don't actually intend to shake paws at first, of course, but people tend to interpret a paw held up or pawing at them as an offer to shake. Shaking is a cute trick, but it also can become annoying or even dangerous (a quick paw to the face can be a serious hazard), so I suggest that if you teach your dog to shake hands, you also teach him to keep his paws on the floor when you say so.

*If your dog naturally holds his paw up, you can teach shake hands by capturing his natural behavior and then adding the command.*

### *Prerequisites and Equipment*

Your dog should sit on command. You need treats and your marker.

215

# TROUBLESHOOTING

## Shake Hands

*Rowdy doesn't like to have his paws held.*

Teach him that having his paws held is okay. Even if you don't care if he learns to shake hands, you do need to handle his paws to trim his nails and check them for injuries from time to time.

Begin by just touching each paw lightly, marking as you touch and then rewarding. If you have to put a leash on your dog to keep him from moving away, do so. As he learns to accept a light touch, progress to putting your fingers lightly around the paw, without squeezing or lifting. Mark and reward while you are touching the paw, then release. When he is comfortable with that much, progress to lifting each paw, mark and reward while you hold the paw, and release. Slowly increase the length of time you hold each paw before you mark, reward, and release. Then progress to lightly massaging each paw. Repeat the process with each paw at least once a day, more often if you can, until your dog is relaxed about having his paws handled.

### Teaching Shake Hands Step By Step

If your dog naturally holds his paw up or taps you with it, you can teach *shake hands* by capturing his natural behavior (see Chapter 5) and then adding the command. You don't need to use treats for a reward in this case, as simply shaking his paw is rewarding.

If your dog does not naturally offer his paw:

1. Have him sit, then lift his paw and gently shake it with one hand, and give him a treat with the other.
2. Repeat a few times.
3. Next, say "Shake" as you lift his paw. He may even begin to offer his paw after getting a few treats.
4. As he gets the idea, stop lifting his paw. Hold your hand out, and if he puts his paw in it, mark and reward. If he doesn't, lightly touch his paw and see if he offers it. If so, mark and treat. If not, go back to lifting it for a few more repetitions, then try again.

### Teaching Paws Off *Step By Step*

*Paws off* is a command I use to mean "put both feet on the floor." This is particularly useful with the dog who likes to paw at people for attention.

One way to teach *paws off* is by capturing:

1. Ignore your dog when he paws at you (don't let him clobber you!), but be ready.
2. The instant that he puts both feet on the floor (he will eventually), mark that behavior.
3. Give him a treat, but do not give it to him if he lifts his paw— wait until he has his paws on the floor again, then instantly pop the treat into his mouth. Timing is critical to be sure that you reward the right behavior.
4. If your dog lifts his paw as you move the treat toward his mouth, either take the treat away or close your hand over it until that foot is back on the ground.

You also can model *paws off* if necessary:

1. If your dog keeps his paw up or taps you with it for longer than you care to wait, or if he is so quick about lifting it that you can't mark and reward while he has it on the floor, gently hold his leg in your hand and move it down until his paw touches

## TROUBLESHOOTING
### Paws Off

*Rowdy has developed the habit of pawing at you.*

Just think of it as a bad habit, and help him break it even if it takes time. In addition to the procedures outlined in this section, you can teach him that pawing at you is counterproductive. When he paws you, get up and ignore him for a moment. Then return and pet him as long as he doesn't paw you. If he starts again, ignore him. If he's never rewarded for the behavior, he'll quit eventually. The problem is, of course, that even if you are consistent, other people will probably reward him for pawing with the attention he wants. So teaching "Paws off" and rewarding him for doing it right in different circumstances is a better choice.

*Some dogs, like this West Highland White Terrier, wave with both paws!*

the floor, then mark and reward, and then release his paw.

2. Repeat several times each session, and keep at it.

## Wave

Teach your dog to wave, and you'll have a real crowd-pleaser.

### *Prerequisites and Equipment*

Your dog should sit, stay, and shake hands on command. You may want to put him on leash for control, and if you use a clicker, you'll need that as well.

### *Teaching* Wave *Step By Step*

1. Have your dog sit, hold out your hand, and tell him "Shake hands."

2. Instead of holding his paw and shaking it, turn your hand palm up and let just his toes rest on your fingertips and lift his paw slightly while you tell him "Wave."

3. Mark and reward while you hold his paw in that position.

4. Repeat several times, then do something else.

5. In your next wave session, repeat the toes-to-fingers routine, but say "Shake wave," then mark and reward while you hold his paw up.

6. When your dog will reach for your hand quickly on the command, pull your hand out of reach as you say "Shake wave," and mark and reward while he has his paw up.

7. When he will raise his paw reliably on command, stop holding your hand out, but continue to mark and reward, every time at first, then sporadically.

8. The final step is to drop the command to shake and simply say "Wave." Too cute!

# TROUBLESHOOTING
## *Wave*

*Rowdy raises his foot sometimes but doesn't seem to know that's what he's supposed to do.*

Be sure that you mark immediately when his foot comes up, even if it's only a little off the ground at first. Timing is critical for teaching the *wave*. As he learns the trick, you can wait until it's finished to give him the reward, but the marker must come at the right time.

## Are You Sleepy? (Play Dead)

This trick can be taught with different commands for different effects. To perform it, your dog will stretch out on his side with his head down as if asleep (or dead, but that doesn't hold much appeal for me).

### Prerequisites and Equipment

Your dog needs to know the *settle* command and must be able to stay still for at least a few seconds. You need your treats, marker, and if necessary, a leash.

### Teaching Are You Sleepy? Step by Step

1. Have your dog settle.
2. With one hand on his shoulder and one on his hip (the one he is not lying on!), gently roll him onto his side. (You may want to kneel on the floor beside your dog to teach this trick—you should be on his "tummy side.")
3. If he doesn't lay his head down, slide your hand up his neck and very gently guide his head and neck to the floor.
4. As soon as he's down flat, mark and reward him.
5. Release him, and repeat several times.
6. The next step is to add the cue. (You can teach your dog to respond the same way to several different cues, but start with just one.) If you plan to use a long phrase, use the final word or two as the cue—"be dead" can be inserted into all sorts

# TROUBLESHOOTING

## *Play Dead*

*Rowdy seems a little nervous about performing this trick, especially around other dogs and strangers.*

Some dogs don't like to perform this trick with other dogs or strangers around because the trick puts them into a very submissive, vulnerable position. Make sure that your dog is very confident about the trick at home before you try it elsewhere, and be sensitive to his emotions when you do. If he seems to be nervous about it, use a different trick to entertain your friends.

of questions. (Would you rather be married or be dead? Be a [political party of choice] or be dead? Be a [dog breed of choice] or be dead?) As long as you stress "be dead," your dog will hear that as his cue.

7. As you begin to roll your dog onto his side, say "Are you sleepy?" or whatever your cue is.

8. Gradually stop rolling him onto his side, but continue to mark and reward him for lying flat.

9. When your dog is very reliable about "going to sleep" from a *settle* position, start teaching him to respond to your cue from a *sit* or *stand*. Begin by giving both commands—"Settle," and as he lies down, "Are you sleepy?" When he's responding quickly to the sequence, eliminate "Settle" so that he "goes to sleep" directly from a *sit* or *stand*. Don't try to rush the process—your dog should respond quickly at each step before you move to the next one.

## Say Your Prayers

This is a good trick to combine with others. You could have your dog say his prayers and go to sleep, for instance. And it's really two tricks in one, because you'll need to teach him "Paws here" first. (Many people teach this as "Paws up" or "Paws on," but "up" and "on" sound a lot like "off," so I use "here" to make it easier for canine ears to distinguish "Paws off" from "Paws here.")

### Prerequisites and Equipment

Your dog should know *stay* in more than one position. It would be helpful, but not necessary, for your dog to know *paws off*. (See section "Shake Hands and Paws Off.") You need treats, your marker, and a leash if your dog is likely to wander away. You also need an elevated surface such as a chair or bed for your dog to rest his paws on. If you want to teach paws here at ground level, you also need something to designate a limited area—like a towel, square of paper, small rug, or hula hoop lying flat.

### Teaching Paws Here Step By Step

1. Sit or stand near the surface where you want your dog to put his paws. You can start with a clearly marked area on the floor or go straight to a chair or bed.
2. Begin by patting the surface to encourage him to put his paw or paws on it.
3. As soon as his paws touch the surface, mark and reward.
4. Repeat several times each session until your dog will put his paws wherever you pat your hand with the *paws here* command.

**Tip:** You can reinforce the *paws off* command while you teach *paws here* by alternating the two. If your *paws here* spot is on the floor or ground, then *paws off* would mean "Step out of the designated area."

### Teaching Say Your Prayers Step by Step

1. Begin with *paws here* on an elevated surface, such as a bed or a chair.

## TROUBLESHOOTING

### Paws Here

*Rowdy sniffs the area you pat but doesn't put his paws on it.*

Model the behavior by lifting his front feet onto the surface.

# TROUBLESHOOTING

## *Say Your Prayers*

*Rowdy tends to step down from the elevated surface as he follows the lure.*

Be sure to keep the lure up at the level of the surface and to move it very slowly. If necessary, steady your dog on the surface with one hand on his back or shoulders. (Just don't push downward—you don't want to push him to the floor).

2. When your dog has both front paws on the spot, use a treat to lure his nose down toward his paws, guiding it so that his forehead ends up near his paws with his nose tucked toward his chest.
3. As you begin to lure him, give your *say your prayers* command.
4. Mark and give him the treat while his head is still tucked in "prayer" position.
5. As your dog responds more and more quickly to the command, begin weaning away the lure, but continue to mark correct behavior and then reward.
6. When he is responding quickly from the *paws here* position, start giving the *say your prayers* command while his feet are still on the ground. Combine it at first with *paws here* so that you're saying "Paws here, say your prayers."
7. When he responds to the two commands by putting his paws on the raised spot and then tucking his head, take away the *paws here* command.

## Where's Your Tail? (Or Wag Your Tail)

I have Australian Shepherds with "nubs" for tails, and people are always saying "Your dog doesn't have a tail." I reply that sure she does, it's small but mighty, and then ask "Where's your tail?", which elicits a lot of nub wagging and butt wriggling. Of course, if your dog has a long tail, you might use "Wag your tail" or "Are you happy?" for this one.

### *Prerequisites and Equipment*

Your dog needs to know how to wag his tail (not usually a problem!), and you need to know how to get him wagging (although that's not usually a problem either). You also need your marker and rewards.

### *Teaching* Where's Your Tail? *Step By Step*

This is a trick best taught by capturing the tail-wagging behavior.

1. Do whatever will make your dog wag his tail—show him a toy, or say "Where's your tail?" in a high-pitched, happy voice.
2. As soon as he wags, mark and reward him. Treats are good rewards, as always, but a nice butt scratch at the base of the tail is perfect for this trick. You also can teach a hand signal (a back-and-forth finger motion is good) by combining the signal with the squeaky voice until your dog will wag for just the signal.

Advanced training, whether in competitive sports or home entertainment, is a wonderful way to enjoy your dog, spend quality time together, exercise his mind and body, and give yourself a sense of achievement.

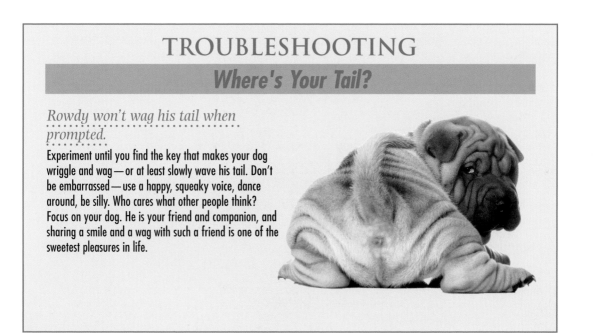

# TROUBLESHOOTING
## Where's Your Tail?

*Rowdy won't wag his tail when prompted.*

Experiment until you find the key that makes your dog wriggle and wag—or at least slowly wave his tail. Don't be embarrassed—use a happy, squeaky voice, dance around, be silly. Who cares what other people think? Focus on your dog. He is your friend and companion, and sharing a smile and a wag with such a friend is one of the sweetest pleasures in life.

**alpha dog:** The socially dominant "top dog" in the hierarchy

**biddability:** A dog's eagerness to do what a human tells him to do

**capturing:** A training approach that reinforces a behavior that a dog performs spontaneously by marking the behavior and rewarding it

**clicker training:** A form of training based on operant conditioning in which the dog learns to associate a marker (in this case, the sound of the click) with a reward

**dominance hierarchy:** A system in which each individual ranks higher or lower in relation to each other animal in a pack

**instincts:** Preprogrammed behaviors or drives that are the result of many generations during which certain behaviors have supported survival of the individual and the species

**luring:** A training approach in which a dog is enticed to perform an action with a reward, usually a treat or toy

**mark:** The act of signaling to a dog to denote a very specific action or behavior

**marker:** A signal, usually auditory but sometimes visual or tactile, that indicates, or marks, a very specific action or behavior

**modeling:** A training approach that involves a person physically positioning or moving a dog to perform an action that the dog will eventually perform on his own

**operant conditioning:** A form of learning in which the dog learns to associate a marker with a reward

**positive reinforcement:** The process of rewarding a dog with something he likes for doing what you want him to do

**primary reinforcer:** A reward that the learner values by nature, like food

**reinforcer:** *See* reward

**reward:** Something that a dog gets as a result of behaving in a certain way. Rewards are used extensively in positive training to motivate learning and occasionally later to reinforce established behaviors.

**secondary reinforcer:** A reward that has acquired value for the learner by being associated with a primary reinforcer

**selective breeding:** The practice of choosing a male and female to mate with as many desirable characteristics and as few undesirable characteristics as possible, in hopes of improving the overall quality of the next generation.

**shaping:** A training approach in which a desired behavior is broken down into tiny increments

**socialization:** The process of learning to get along socially with other dogs

**targeting:** A training approach that teaches a dog to touch a specific object to earn a reward (a treat at first, then verbal rewards punctuated by occasional treats)

**temperament:** A dog's fundamental tendency to display friendliness, reserve, aggression, stability, and other traits

# ASSOCIATIONS AND ORGANIZATIONS

## REGISTRIES

### American Kennel Club (AKC)
5580 Centerview Drive
Raleigh, NC 27606
Telephone: (919) 233-9767
Fax: (919) 233-3627
E-mail: info@akc.org
www.akc.org

### Canadian Kennel Club (CKC)
89 Skyway Avenue, Suite 100
Etobicoke, Ontario M9W 6R4
Telephone: (416) 675-5511
Fax: (416) 675-6506
E-mail: information@ckc.ca
www.ckc.ca

### The Kennel Club
1 Clarges Street
London
W1J 8AB
Telephone: 0870 606 6750
Fax: 0207 518 1058
www.the-kennel-club.org.uk

### United Kennel Club (UKC)
100 E. Kilgore Road
Kalamazoo, MI 49002-5584
Telephone: (269) 343-9020
Fax: (269) 343-7037
E-mail: pbickell@ukcdogs.com
www.ukcdogs.com

# RESCUE ORGANIZATIONS AND ANIMAL WELFARE GROUPS

### American Humane Association (AHA)
63 Inverness Drive East
Englewood, CO 80112
Telephone: (303) 792-9900
Fax: 792-5333
www.americanhumane.org

### American Society for the Prevention of Cruelty to Animals (ASPCA)
424 E. 92nd Street
New York, NY 10128-6804
Telephone: (212) 876-7700
www.aspca.org

### Royal Society for the Prevention of Cruelty to Animals (RSPCA)
Telephone: 0870 3335 999
Fax: 0870 7530 284
www.rspca.org.uk

### The Humane Society of the United States (HSUS)
2100 L Street, NW
Washington DC 20037
Telephone: (202) 452-1100
www.hsus.org

## Sports

**American Kennel Club**

*Agility:* www.akc.org/ events/agility/index.cfm

*Conformation:* www.akc. org/events/conformation/ index.cfm

*Obedience:* www.akc.org/ events/obedience/index. cfm

*Rally:* www.akc.org/ events/rally/index.cfm

*Tracking:* www.akc.org/ events/tracking/index.cfm

**American Herding Breeds Association (AHBA)**

www.ahba-herding.org

**American Mixed Breed Obedience Registry (AMBOR)**

www.amborusa.com

**Association of Pet Dog Trainers (APDT) Rally**

www.apdt.com/po/rally/ default.aspx

**International Agility Link (IAL)**

www.agilityclick.com/~ial

**North American Dog Agility Council (NADAC)**

www.nadac.com

**North American Flyball Association (NAFA)**

www.flyball.org

**United States Dog Agility Association (USDAA)**

www.usdaa.com

## Veterinary Resources

**Academy of Veterinary Homeopathy (AVH)**

P.O. Box 9280

Wilmington, DE 19809

Telephone: (866) 652-1590

Fax: (866) 652-1590

E-mail: office@TheAVH.org

www.theavh.org

**American Academy of Veterinary Acupuncture (AAVA)**

100 Roscommon Drive, Suite 320

Middletown, CT 06457

Telephone: (860) 635-6300

Fax: (860) 635-6400

E-mail: office@aava.org

www.aava.org

**American Animal Hospital Association (AAHA)**

P.O. Box 150899

Denver, CO 80215-0899

Telephone: (303) 986-2800

Fax: (303) 986-1700

E-mail: info@aahanet.org

www.aahanet.org/index. cfm

**American Holistic Veterinary Medical Association (AHVMA)**

2218 Old Emmorton Road

Bel Air, MD 21015

Telephone: (410) 569-0795

Fax: (410) 569-2346

E-mail: office@ahvma.org

www.ahvma.org

**American Veterinary Medical Association (AVMA)**

1931 North Meacham Road – Suite 100

Schaumburg, IL 60173

Telephone: (847) 925-8070

Fax: (847) 925-1329

E-mail: avmainfo@avma.org

www.avma.org

**British Veterinary Association (BVA)**

7 Mansfield Street

London

W1G 9NQ

Telephone: 020 7636 6541

Fax: 020 7436 2970

E-mail: bvahq@bva.co.uk

www.bva.co.uk

## TRAINING AND BEHAVIOR RESOURCES

### Animal Behavior Society (ABS)

Certified Applied Animal Behaviorist Directory: www.animalbehavior.org/ABSAppliedBehavior/caab-directory

### Association of Pet Dog Trainers (APDT)

150 Executive Center Drive
Box 35
Greenville, SC 29615
Telephone: (800) PET-DOGS
Fax: (864) 331-0767
E-mail: information@apdt.com
www.apdt.com

### Certification Council for Professional Dog Trainers (CCPDT)

E-mail: administrator@ccpdt.org
www.ccpdt.org

## ANIMAL-ASSISTED ACTIVITIES & THERAPY ORGANIZATIONS

### Delta Society

875 124th Ave NE, Suite 101
Bellevue, WA 98005
Telephone: (425) 226-7357
Fax: (425) 235-1076
E-mail: info@deltasociety.org
www.deltasociety.org

### Therapy Dogs, Inc.

P.O. Box 20227
Cheyenne WY 82003
Telephone: 877-843-7364
E-mail: therapydogsinc@qwest.net
www.therapydogs.com

### Therapy Dogs International, Inc. (TDI)

88 Bartley Road
Flanders, NJ 07836
Telephone: (973) 252-9800
Fax: (973) 252-7171
E-mail: tdi@gti.net
www.tdi-dog.org

## PUBLICATIONS

### BOOKS

Anderson, Teoti. Terra-Nova *Puppy Care & Training.* Neptune City: T.F.H. Publications, Inc., 2007.

———. *The Super Simple Guide to Housetraining.* Neptune City: T.F.H. Publications, Inc., 2004.

De Vito, Dominique. Animal Planet *Training Your Dog.* Neptune City: T.F.H. Publications, Inc., 2007.

King, Trish. *Parenting Your Dog.* Neptune City: T.F.H. Publications, Inc., 2004.

Yin, Sophia. *How to Behave so Your Dog Behaves.* T.F.H. Publications, Inc., 2004.

### MAGAZINES

### AKC Family Dog

American Kennel Club
260 Madison Avenue
New York, NY 10016
Telephone: (800) 490-5675
E-mail: familydog@akc.org
www.akc.org/pubs/familydog

### AKC Gazette

American Kennel Club
260 Madison Avenue
New York, NY 10016
Telephone: (800) 533-7323
E-mail: gazette@akc.org
www.akc.org/pubs/gazette

### Dog & Kennel

Pet Publishing, Inc.
7-L Dundas Circle
Greensboro, NC 27407
Telephone: (336) 292-4272
Fax: (336) 292-4272
E-mail: info@petpublishing.com
www.dogandkennel.com

**Dog Fancy**

Subscription Department
P.O. Box 53264
Boulder, CO 80322-3264
Telephone: (800) 365-4421
E-mail: barkback@dogfancy.com
www.dogfancy.com

**Dogs Monthly**

Ascot House
High Street, Ascot,
Berkshire SL5 7JG
United Kingdom
Telephone: 0870 730 8433
Fax: 0870 730 8431
E-mail: admin@rtc-associates.freeserve.co.uk
www.corsini.co.uk/dogsmonthly

www.nylabone.com
www.tfh.com

Note: **Boldfaced** numbers indicate
illustrations.

INDEX

Adrian Moisei (Shutterstock): 196

AioK (Shutterstock): 98

Alexey Stiop (Shutterstock): 229

Annette (Shutterstock): 139, 168

April Turner (Shutterstock): 47

Bianca Lagalla (Shutterstock): 172

Brian Finestone (Shutterstock): 10

Casey K. Bishop (Shutterstock): 113

Chin Kit Sen (Shutterstock): 181

Chris Bence (Shutterstock): 45

Chris Mathews (Shutterstock): 81

Cindy Hughes (Shutterstock): 38

Claudia Steininger (Shutterstock): 119

Condor 36 (Shutterstock): 125

Costin Cojocaru (Shutterstock): 70, 174

Dana Bartekoske (Shutterstock): 190

Denis Tabler (Shutterstock): 160

Devin Koob (Shutterstock): 68 (middle)

Doghouse Arts: 202

Dumitrescu Ciprian-Florin (Shutterstock): 108

Dusan Po (Shutterstock): 131

Elliot Westacott (Shutterstock): 130, 162, 226

Eric Isselée (Shutterstock): front cover, 15, 27 (bottom), 29, 30, 31, 80 (left), 93, 105, 121, 142, 170, 173 (bottom), 201, 223, 225

Erik Lam (Shutterstock): 50, 136 (box), 212, 215, 217, 220

Frank-Peter Funke (Shutterstock): 153

Galina Barskaya (Shutterstock): 4, 21

Gelpi (Shutterstock): 148, 221 (box)

Gertjan Hooijer (Shutterstock): 210

Graca Victoria (Shutterstock): 24

iofoto (Shutterstock): 167 (bottom), 221 (top)

Ivonne Wierink (Shutterstock): 63

Izim M. Gulcuk (Shutterstock): 20

Jaimie Duplass (Shutterstock): 7, 8 (sidebar), 16, 22, 23, 37, 43, 55, 65, 86, 112, 136 (left sidebar), 138, 164 (sidebar), 167 (sidebar), 173 (sidebar), 178 (sidebar), 188, 211 (bottom sidebar), spine

Jason Osborne (Shutterstock): 161

jean morrison (Shutterstock): 146

Jennifer Sekerka (Shutterstock): 40

Jonathan Pais (Shutterstock): 104

Joy Brown (Shutterstock): 69 (bottom)

JP (Shutterstock): back cover (bottom)

Judy Ben Joud (Shutterstock): 101

K Chelette (Shutterstock): 183

Katrina Brown (Shutterstock): 14, 27 (sidebar), 39, 42, 46, 57, 73, 76, 89, 92, 95, 109, 115, 118, 120, 126 (sidebar), 141, 144, 147, 163 (sidebar), 179, 180, 195 (sidebar), 197, 205, 209, 211 (top sidebar)

Kerioak-Christine Nichols (Shutterstock): 158

Lars Christensen (Shutterstock): 116, 189

Laurent Laurant (Shutterstock): back cover (top)

Leonid V. Kruzhkov (Shutterstock): 66 (top)

Lindsay Dean (Shutterstock): 102

Lynn Watson (Shutterstock): 60

MAGDALENA SZACHOWSKA (Shutterstock): 99

Marcy J. Levinson (Shutterstock): 69 (top)

Michael Ledray (Shutterstock): 84

Michael Pettigrew (Shutterstock): 18, 163, 219

N Joy Neish (Shutterstock): 132

Nancy Clemons (Shutterstock): 56

Nicholas James Homrich (Shutterstock): 165

Patrick McCall (Shutterstock): 91

Paul S. Wolf (Shutterstock): 126 (top)

Paulette Braun: 44, 51, 53

Phil Date (Shutterstock): 28, 78, 216

Photomediacom (Shutterstock): 32

Pieter (Shutterstock): 150, 151, 214

pixshots (Shutterstock): 79

Premier Pet Products: 67 (top)

Rick's Photography (Shutterstock): 222

Rix Pix (Shutterstock): 3, 35, 87, 100, 135 (sidebar), 157, 171, 194

Robynrg (Shutterstock): 83, 199

Ronnie Howard (Shutterstock): 177

Shawn Hine (Shutterstock): 106

Shutterstock: 127

Somer McCain (Shutterstock): 68 (bottom)

Suponev Vladimir Mihajlovich (Shutterstock): 128

Tad Denson (Shutterstock): 26, 111, 129, 186, 193

teekaygee (Shutterstock): back cover (top)

Terry Leong (Shutterstock): 231

Thomas Bedenk (Shutterstock): 166

Tina Rencelj (Shutterstock): 134, 154

Tommy Maenhout (Shutterstock): 58

Tootles (Shutterstock): 75, 178 (bottom)

troy (Shutterstock): 204

verity Johnson (Shutterstock): 77

WizData, inc. (Shutterstock): 137

Yuri Arcurs (Shutterstock): 152

Zoom Team (Shutterstock): 59

All other photos courtesy of Isabelle Francais and T.F.H. archives.

# DEDICATION

For Roger, and the dogs.

# ACKNOWLEDGEMENTS

I couldn't begin to acknowledge by name all the individuals who taught me and shaped my thinking about dog training, but I do thank all the instructors, writers, trainers, competitors, and dog owners I've encountered on this journey. Thanks also to Stephanie Fornino, my astute editor at T.F.H.—it's been a pleasure, as always! And of course the dogs, always and forever, the dogs.

# ABOUT THE AUTHOR

**Sheila Webster Boneham, Ph.D.**, loves dogs and writing about dogs. Three of her books have won the prestigious Maxwell Award from the Dog Writers Association of America, including *The Simple Guide to Labrador Retrievers*, named Best Single Breed Book of 2002. For the past decade, Sheila has taught people about dogs through her writing and other activities. She hopes that her successes and mistakes as a puppy buyer, breeder, trainer, owner, and rescuer can benefit other dog lovers and their dogs. Sheila and her canine companions are active in competition and in dog-assisted activities and therapy. A former university writing teacher, Sheila also conducts writing workshops. You can visit Sheila and her dogs on the web at www.sheilaboneham.com.

# Nylabone® Cares.

Millions of dogs of all ages, breeds, and sizes have enjoyed our world-famous chew bones—but we're not just bones! Nylabone®, the leader in responsible animal care for over 50 years, devotes the same care and attention to our many other award-winning, high-quality, innovative products. Your dog will love them — and so will you!

Toys     Edibles     Chews     Crates

Available at retailers everywhere. Visit us online at www.nylabone.com